HOW TO NOT ANNOY THE JUDGE

A GUIDE TO: RIDE SMARTER. SHOW SHARPER. WIN BIGGER.

ALLISON DEARDORFF

HOW TO NOT ANNOY THE JUDGE
A GUIDE TO: RIDE SMARTER.
SHOW SHARPER. WIN BIGGER.

Copyright © 2026 by Allison Deardorff

All rights reserved. No part of this book may be reproduced in any form or by any electronic or mechanical means, including information storage and retrieval systems, without written permission from the author, except for the use of brief quotations in a book review.

Disclaimer:

The author has personally applied and observed the principles discussed in this book; however, no claims, promises, or guarantees are made regarding results, performance, or safety. The information provided is intended for educational purposes only and is not a substitute for appropriate professional instruction, coaching, or supervision.

By choosing to apply any concepts or strategies discussed in this book, the reader assumes full responsibility for their decisions and actions. The author shall not be held liable for any injury, loss, or damage arising from the use or misuse of the information contained herein.

ISBN: 979-8-9947418-1-8

Cover Photographer: Howard Schatzberg

Cover Designer: Saddlethreads

DEDICATION

For my father, Don Deardorff,
my toughest critic and my greatest supporter.

For my husband, Marc Hevern,
who never blinked when I said I was going to write a book or at any of my ambitious/unconventional ideas.

For the horses,
who have literally shaped my life and career.

And for the show ring,
for the tough love, the meaningful rewards and the clarity of purpose it demands.

TABLE OF CONTENTS

Introduction	7
1. The Judge's Perspective and Why This Book Exists	12
2. The Truth Behind the Clipboard	17
3. When the Judges' Cards Look "All Over the Place"	24
4. Judging Your Friends and Foes	29
5. Let's Talk About It. Politics in Judged Competitions	35
6. This Is Not a Fashion Show (Though I Love the Gowns)	43
7. The Winner's Mindset	51
8. Belief Is A Muscle	61
9. We Can't All Be Jordan (Or Tom Moore) And That's Ok	69
10. Outriding Fear And Why Owning It Is the Fastest Way Forward	76
11. How Champions Enter and How to Break Through What's Holding You Back	82
12. The Walk. Planning, Positioning, and Not Losing the Class	92
13. The Reverse, The Reveal	99
14. How to Show Like You Planned It	113
15. Equitation. Every Detail Matters	121
16. Yes, the Judging Is Over, But...	130
17. Losing Loudly, Learning Quietly	138
18. Presentation and Preparation Are Part of the Performance	148
19. Beyond the Ribbon. Riding for More	161
20. Study the Game	173
21. Feel Is Earned	186
22. The Coachability Factor	194
23. Lessons Learned	205

24. Consistency Counts More Than the Highlight Reel	214
25. Judges in the Wild (and Other Moments You're Still Being Judged)	219
26. Contacting Judges After the Show. When (and How) to Ask for Feedback	226
27. It's Just a Horse Show. When Disagreeing With the Judge Goes Too Far	232
28. Rail Distractions, Coaching, Cheering, and Crossing the Line	239
29. You're Not Showing Alone And How the Entire Ecosystem Impacts the Ride	246
30. Be a Good Human. It Pays Off.	252
31. When the Horse Doesn't Fit. Why Letting Go Is Sometimes the Smartest Move	257
32. They'll Never Get It And That's Okay	267
33. What Doesn't Annoy the Judge (And Might Even Earn You Respect)	272
34. Center Ring Secrets	276
35. What Comes Next	288
Acknowledgments	293
About the Author	295
Appendix	299

INTRODUCTION

If you're holding this book, you're already ahead of most riders. You're not just showing up, you're here to improve. That mindset makes you a competitor. You want more than a decent ride. You want to win. And you're wise enough to know that something small but important might be standing between you and consistent, undeniable success. This kind of awareness is what separates the ambitious from the average. Welcome. You just gave yourself an edge.

This isn't a riding lesson. I'm not here to break down leads, diagonals, or headset mechanics. I won't tell you how to train a horse either. If you picked up this book, I'm assuming you already know the basics and probably a lot more. What we *are* going to talk about are the subtle elements many people don't realize make a big difference in the show ring. The things that can make or break your performance and your placing in a judged sport.

Plenty of riders can win once, but true champions win consistently regardless of the arena, the competition, or the circumstances. That kind of success isn't built on talent alone.

It's built on poise, timing, presence, and an understanding of the silent signals that tip the scales when it matters most.

Horse showing is hard enough. Why make it harder by unknowingly annoying the judge? I've stood in the center ring for years, watching talented riders lose ribbons over fixable details. There is good news though. Most of what makes a strong impression on a judge isn't about talent. It's about awareness. Once you know what judges actually look for and what quietly drives them crazy, you'll enter the ring with more confidence, more consistency, and more control over your outcomes.

Yes, talent matters and so does top notch training. And of course, a high-quality horse wearing beautiful tack doesn't hurt. However, those aren't the whole story, they are just part of the picture. The riders who win again and again pay attention to the things we don't always openly discuss. Until now.

As a USEF judge with licenses in American Saddlebreds, Hackneys, Roadsters, Saddle Seat Equitation, and Morgans, I've officiated some of the most prestigious events in our sport as well as local level shows. I've judged the Morgan Grand National, the South African National Championship Horse Show, and the World's Championship Horse Show. I've also trained World and National Champions, Saddle Seat World Cup team members, coached amateurs and junior exhibitors into the winner's circle, and seen firsthand what really moves the needle and what doesn't. I've also lost, at every level, sometimes narrowly, sometimes painfully, with exceptional horses and riders. That perspective matters, because the difference between winning and not winning is rarely luck and almost never accidental.

This book isn't about quick fixes or recycled advice. It's an insider's guide to what actually influences a judge when it's time to split hairs. You'll learn how to build ring presence, avoid subtle missteps, and showcase your best self and horse under pressure. We will talk about mindset, ringsmanship, and the intangibles that make you memorable for the right reasons.

Honestly, winning in the show ring isn't just about having the most expensive horse or a custom suit. It's not even about being the most technically skilled rider. We've all seen it, a seemingly "average" team takes home the blue ribbon, not because they out-rode everyone, but because they out-showed them. It's not luck. It's a strategy.

If you want to win more, it's time to start riding like you're being judged. Because you are.

Allison, judging the UPHA Chapter Five Horse Show. Photo by Howard Schatzberg.

HOW TO USE THIS BOOK

This book is not meant to be read one rigid way.

You can read it cover to cover. You can jump straight to the chapter that applies to the class, horse, or problem you're dealing with right now. You can come back to certain sections again and again as your riding, goals, and perspective evolve.

Each chapter is designed to stand on its own. That has been done intentionally. Horse showing is not linear, and neither is improvement. What you need before your first rated show is different from what you need when you're chasing a championship or rebuilding confidence after a rough season.

Use this book the way it serves you best.

My entire life and career have been spent competing, training, and judging in the Saddlebred, Hackney, Roadster and Morgan worlds. Naturally, many of the stories and examples come from those disciplines. That is the arena I know best, and I do not pretend otherwise.

That said, most of the principles behind the examples are not breed-specific. They can be applied to any judged sport or competition.

Judges evaluate presence, preparation, consistency, decision-making, and professionalism the same way across disciplines. The mechanics may change, but the expectations do not. I have intentionally written many of these lessons so they translate beyond my chosen discipline and into hunters, dressage, stock and western horses, other gaited breeds, and more.

And interestingly, some of these concepts reach even

further. I have had dog show competitors tell me they recognized the same judging dynamics, ring psychology, and competitive patterns in their own sport.

If you ride a different breed or discipline, please do not get stuck on the details. Focus on the mindset, the strategy, and the patterns. That is where the value is. The ring may look different. The rules may change. The judge and human nature does not.

You'll also notice that certain themes and ideas show up more than once. It's not just filler. The fundamentals matter, and the things that actually influence judges, outcomes, and perception are often the same things exhibitors overlook. Repetition drives the point home, because in the show ring, small habits repeated consistently are what separate average rides from winning ones.

Underline. Dog-ear pages. Make notes in the margins. Come back to sections before a big show or a big event. This isn't a book you read once and shelve. It's a reference, a reset, and sometimes a reality check.

Most of all, use it as a tool. Not to ride like someone else, but to ride with more awareness, confidence, and purpose. The goal of this book is simple. To help you become the best equestrian you are capable of being, on any horse, in any ring, on any day.

1

THE JUDGE'S PERSPECTIVE AND WHY THIS BOOK EXISTS

Let's get one thing straight right out of the gate. Judges are not lurking in center ring waiting to take you down. Not to age myself, but I have been judging for about twenty-five years. If anything, I'm hoping every single horse that trots through that gate makes my job harder by putting in a performance of a lifetime. Most of us are horse-obsessed, detail-driven perfectionists who genuinely want to see horses and riders rise to the moment. And that is exactly why this book exists.

What most exhibitors don't realize is how much responsibility comes with judging. Every class requires instant decisions backed by rules, class specifications, consistency, and fairness. Judges are processing dozens of variables at once, way of going, correctness, execution, ring awareness, presentation, manners, timing, and how well horse and rider meet the expectations of that specific class. There is no rewind button. There is no slow motion. We make calls in real time, under pressure, knowing that every ribbon matters deeply to someone.

This is not a guide on which tack to buy, what color coat is in style, or how to fix your horse in thirty days. This is the insider manual riders rarely get. It is the separation line between good and great. It is the attitude, the awareness, the timing, the presence, and the strategy that turn potential into blue ribbons. I want to share the details that get overlooked or that no one ever explained.

Most riders are working hard. The issue is that hard work without direction turns into guesswork and that leads to frustration. Frustration leads to burnout or blame. This book exists to replace guessing with understanding. When you understand how you are being evaluated, your preparation changes. Your confidence changes. Your ability to recover from a mistake changes. And yes, your results change.

Why write it now? Because the demand finally slapped me in the face. In February 2025, I taught at the infamous High Caliber Stables Adult Clinic put on by Evan and Mary Orr. Mary, who sees talent and opportunity better than almost anyone, knew I would thrive teaching from the judge's perspective in real time. The second I started sharing what judges actually see and actually think, the questions exploded. Riders wanted real answers. They wanted the truth. And they wanted it from someone who had lived it in the center of the ring.

What struck me most during that clinic was how many riders had never thought of these things in this way before. Not because trainers were withholding information, but because much of it lives in experience, not instruction. Judges do not announce what they are thinking. Riders rarely get feedback from the judge's perspective unless something goes wrong. This creates a massive gap between effort and understanding. That gap is where confidence erodes and resentment grows.

That weekend sent me home fired up. I opened my laptop and started writing for the riders who deserved clarity. Then I decided to start posting on social media on the subject. The more I shared, the more I realized that many exhibitors had been guessing for much of their horse-showing lives. It became obvious that riders are hungry for straight forward and not watered down information that helps them actually improve and understand their placings from the judge's perspective.

The response confirmed what I had suspected for years. There is an unspoken curriculum in this sport. The riders who rise to the top tend to learn it quietly, over time, through observation, mentorship, and sometimes painful trial and error. This book is about accelerating that learning curve without sacrificing integrity, sportsmanship, or horsemanship.

"NOT ANNOYED. JUST INVESTED."

A few months into writing this book, I got a call from a fellow trainer and judge whom I respect. He's known for his work ethic, his dedication to the breed, and his commitment to always telling it like it is. I won't name him here, though he might choose to reveal himself at some point, but his feedback ended up being more useful than he probably intended. He opened the conversation with: "I've been reading your judging stuff on Facebook...and to be honest, I don't agree with all of it." I kind of laughed and replied, "Oh yeah?" He went on to say something I completely agree with and actually try to embody every time I step into the ring with my clipboard: "I don't think it's our job to stand out there and be annoyed. It's our job to pick nice horses and encourage people to keep trying." He's right.

What I realized in that moment was that I've been using the word "annoy" as a hook, to start conversations, shake people up a little, and get their attention. It's a blunt word. And while it works for social media to make people stop scrolling, it does not paint the full picture. So let me clarify here, in the right context, I am not annoyed to be judging horses. I'm honored. I get to watch from the best seat in the house. I get to assess riders, drivers, and trainers I've admired since I was a kid, some of whom I still aspire to ride like. I get to witness the first brave steps of a rookie amateur, a tiny walk and trot rider's debut and the first trip off the farm for a young horse. These are moments I take seriously. I never forget the privilege of being in that center ring.

Yes, there are times when I get frustrated when something preventable interferes with the outcome of a class and keeps the best horse from winning. A mistimed transition, a rider who freezes under pressure, a spectator who squeaks their chair at the exact wrong moment. It's not irritation for the sake of it, it's disappointment because I want to get it right. I want to reward the best performance, and I want every rider and horse to have the opportunity to be that best performance. That phone call helped me refine how I talk about judging, not just online, but in this book.

The truth is, this project isn't about criticism or clever phrasing. It's about pulling back the curtain and making this sport less mysterious and more fair. It's about helping riders and trainers understand what's actually happening in the ring and giving them a better chance to rise to the occasion. Transparency doesn't weaken this sport. It strengthens it. And the more we understand about showing and judging, the better we all become.

So to the friend who picked up the phone and challenged my wording I want to say thank you. You helped me clarify my intention.

What I love most is helping people win, in whatever way winning looks for them. Maybe it is roses on the green shavings. Maybe it is leaving your class without feeling like you're going to cry in the tack room. I've judged the biggest shows in our industry, watched legends get made, and watched riders drag themselves back from disaster to deliver the ride of their career. If there is a major class in this country, odds are I've judged it, shown in it, or coached someone who got a ribbon in it.

I have also watched incredibly capable riders consistently miss opportunities simply because they did not understand how the class unfolded from the judge's vantage point. Small choices compound. Awareness compounds. Presence compounds. The goal is not perfection. The goal is intention paired with knowledge.

Along the way, I've collected more pet peeves, jaw-dropping moments, and "what exactly was that?" stories than I can count. And some of are about me. As long as you promise not to recreate some of them in your next class.

Those stories are not meant to embarrass anyone. They exist to teach. Every mistake you will read about has been made by someone who cared deeply and tried hard. The difference between riders who repeat those mistakes and riders who grow past them is understanding.

Think of this book as your playbook. Your edge. Your chance to understand what the judge sees long before the lineup. Use it to sharpen your instincts, elevate your presence, and make sure the judge is rooting for you the second you step into the ring.

Ready to become unforgettable? Let's get started.

2

THE TRUTH BEHIND THE CLIPBOARD

JUDGING MYTHS, DEBUNKED

Before we go any further, we need to clear up a few things. No, judges don't get paid off. No, we're not handing out ribbons to our friends or just because we like someone's outfit. I've heard it all, half-whispers behind the barn, Facebook post rants, conspiracy theories that would make the Illuminati blush. Much of what people *think* they know about judging is wrong. And if you want to win, you'd better start understanding what actually matters in the center ring.

When you spend your career on both sides of the clipboard, as a competitor and a judge, you realize just how wide the gap is between what people believe is happening and what's actually going on. This chapter exists to close that gap. Not with sugarcoating, but with facts.

1. "IT'S ALL POLITICS."

We've all heard it. And sure reputation, consistency, and presence can influence how a horse or rider is perceived over time.

That's true in *every* judged sport. But the idea that a judge walks into the ring with a pre-written card? That's just lazy thinking. There's no backroom deal. No secret alliance. Just a bunch of horses going head-to-head and someone has to sort them.

The best way to beat politics, either real or perceived, is to make your performance so sharp, so dialed-in, so far above the rest that it makes the decision easy. Be undeniable.

2. "JUDGES GET PAID OFF."

This myth is the horse show world's version of a Bigfoot sighting. It makes for juicy gossip, but it's not rooted in reality. We don't risk our careers, reputations, or licenses over a ribbon.

Instead, sometimes we get paid in complaints, emails, Facebook shade. And maybe a water bottle if we're lucky. That's the glamour of judging.

Joking aside, licensed judging requires integrity, training and scrutiny. The vast majority of judges I've worked with take the responsibility seriously because we love the sport and want to see it flourish.

3. "JUDGES ALWAYS PLACE THEIR FRIENDS HIGHER."

Actually, the opposite is often true. Most judges go *out of their way* to avoid even the appearance of favoritism. If we know you personally, we're often harder on you in an attempt to protect our own credibility.

I've judged horses I know and love and still tied them second or third because they didn't win *that day*. We're trained to separate emotion from evaluation. It's not always easy, but it's part of the job.

4. "THE JUDGES DON'T REMEMBER MY HORSE."

We remember more than you think, but you want to be memorable for the right reasons. A consistent, well-prepared horse with a polished ride will stick in our minds a lot longer than the one with a glitter bomb for a browband and a sloppy performance to match.

If you show up clean, confident, and consistent at every show, not just the big ones, you'll start building a reputation that sticks. But it's a slow build, not a one-and-done deal.

5. "ONCE A JUDGE DOESN'T LIKE YOU, YOU'RE DOOMED."

Nope. This isn't high school, and we're not holding grudges. Most judges want every rider to show improvement. We *want* to see you come back stronger.

I've judged riders who completely missed the mark at one show and, several months later, returned far more connected with the same horse, riding smarter, presenting the horse more effectively, and placing right at the top. It isn't personal. It's performance.

That means you can recover, rebuild, and return with a new ride and a new outcome. But you have to let go of the idea that your past defines your future in the ring.

6. "JUDGES CAN'T TELL WHEN A HORSE IS PACING."

Oh, we can tell. Trust me, we can *always* tell. A horse that is pacing instead of slow gaiting or racking sticks out like a sore thumb to any trained eye. We just don't always have a better option.

Sometimes, that pacing horse is still the best one in the class. Maybe the others have no motion. Maybe they made too many mistakes. Maybe their trots are weak, their necks are straight, or their gaits are inconsistent. We can only judge what's in front of us and that is the actual reality of holding the judge's card.

And in a five-gaited class, we're not just judging the slow gait and rack, we're evaluating *all five gaits*. *It's not about one perfect gait, it's about the best overall performance that day.*

7. "MY TRAINER SAID WE SHOULD'VE WON, SO THE JUDGE MUST BE WRONG."

Your trainer sees it from the rail. We see it from the middle of the ring. Different angles, different vantage points, and a whole different perspective.

It's not that your trainer is wrong, they just aren't judging. They're coaching. Their job is to help *you* get better. Our job is to rank everyone fairly.

And sometimes those jobs come to two different conclusions.

8. "JUDGES PREFER CERTAIN BLOODLINES OR TRAINERS."

Judges don't care who trained your horse or what its pedigree says if it doesn't perform. Yes, some barns consistently win, but it's usually because they consistently produce prepared, quality horses, not because of favoritism.

What looks like "barn bias" is often just preparation bias. When you see a horse that enters the ring with presence, power, manners, and motion, *that's* what's catching our eye.

It's not about your last name. It's about your last pass.

9. "JUDGES ARE BIASED AGAINST HORSES OF COLOR."

Whether it's a pinto, palomino, gray, or anything outside the classic bay or chestnut, some people assume colored horses don't win because of how they look.

The truth is we don't care what color your horse is. We care if it's good. Period.

Some of the best horses I've ever tied were pinto, grey, etc. If a colored horse isn't placing, it's not because of its color, it's because something else didn't stack up that day. A great one will get noticed, no matter the paint job.

10. "IF I DIDN'T PLACE, I MUST'VE DONE SOMETHING WRONG."

Not always. Sometimes, it's just that someone else did something *better*. This is a judged sport, it's comparative.

Your ride may have been solid, but if someone else had more presence, better expression, or simply a better moment when it counted, that's what tips the scale.

It's not about being perfect. It's about being the most right, the most ready, and the most polished on that day, in that moment.

That's why second place doesn't mean failure, it just means someone edged you out. And that's the kind of challenge that should fuel your fire.

JUDGING WHILE HUMAN

We don't talk enough about the reality that judges are human beings. We're expected to perform under pressure just like riders. And sometimes, we mess up.

One of my most embarrassing moments of my judging career happened in a class where two riders came in wearing nearly identical maroon coats. Both were riding chestnut horses. One of them had an undeniably brilliant trip; first place without question. The other had some trouble during the class and should've been at the bottom.

But I had something in my eye that day. I could barely keep it open, let alone see clearly through it. I kept blinking, trying to work around it, thinking I could push through. In the lineup, I confused the two numbers. I placed the rider who should have been last in first, and the one who earned the win at the bottom of the card.

As soon as I realized what I'd done, my heart sank. I was mortified. After the show, I found both trainers and apologized. They were gracious and understanding, but that didn't make it easier. I had let them down, and worse, I had let myself down. I've never forgotten it.

Judging carries weight. When we make mistakes, we carry them long after the crowd has moved on. But in the ring, we don't get the luxury of explaining ourselves in real time. We make the best calls we can with the information and conditions we have in the moment and sometimes, that moment is harder than it looks.

THE EMOTIONAL TOLL OF HIGH-STAKES SEASONS

This isn't just about judges. Riders, trainers, owners, everyone involved in this sport feels the toll of a long, high-pressure show season.

You may be:

- Burned out.
- Questioning your worth.
- Wondering if this is the year it finally comes together or the year it all slips through your fingers.

Let me say this clearly, **judges feel it too.** You don't always see the fatigue behind the clipboard. You don't always see the self-doubt that creeps in when we have to make a tough call in a deep class. You don't see the nights we lie awake hoping we made the right decision, knowing someone's whole season may have hinged on it. No one is immune. Not even the people handing out the trophies. Being "almost ready" is a beautiful place for progress but a terrible place to park your dreams. The judges can feel it. So can your horse. So can you.

FINAL THOUGHTS

The truth is, judging isn't as mysterious as people make it out to be. It's not perfect, but it *is* deliberate. Most of us take the job seriously, lose sleep over close calls, and care deeply about doing right by the horses, the riders, and the sport.

We don't get it right 100% of the time. But we're trying. Every class, every show, every decision, we're trying.

If you want to succeed in this sport, start by tossing out the myths. They're not helping you. They're clouding your thinking and giving you an excuse to stop improving.

Don't let made-up stories block you from getting better. Learn the real rules, then go out there and play the game like someone who came to win.

3

WHEN THE JUDGES' CARDS LOOK "ALL OVER THE PLACE"

We've all heard it: *"Those cards were all over the place, what were they watching out there?"*

It is one of the most common complaints ringside, and I understand why. To an exhibitor or a trainer, seeing one judge put you at the top and another bury you can feel infuriating. Parents and clients who do not understand the system often jump to the conclusion that the judging was ignored them or they were biased. The truth is, in many cases, that's actually the system working exactly as it was designed.

WHY CARDS DON'T MATCH

A three-judge panel is not meant to produce identical cards, though sometimes it does. It is meant to produce an accurate average of different, independent opinions. If all three judges had the same card all the time, we wouldn't need three judges in the first place. The point is to reduce the chance that one mistake, one blind spot, or one personal preference will control the outcome.

When you see spreads like a 1-1-8 or a 1-5-8, it doesn't mean someone was asleep during the class. It usually means they saw different things. And if you've ever judged, you know just how easy it is to see something no one else did.

JUDGES WATCH DIFFERENT ANGLES

Judges are not always watching the exact same thing at the exact same time and that is the point. One may be locked in on a horse in front of center ring, while another is scanning the far end of the arena, and the third is focused on the other rail.

Imagine a horse making a near-perfect pass down the rail in front of Judge A. Judge B is across the ring and sees the same horse break stride on the end. Judge C is looking at another entry at that moment and never notices either moment. Same horse. Same class. Three sets of eyes, three different realities. To the audience, it looks like "the cards are all over the place." To the judges, it looks like honest observation from different vantage points.

HORSES SHOW THEIR GOOD AND BAD SIDES

Every horse, no matter how elite, has strengths and weaknesses. A powerful trot the first way of the ring may flatten the second way. A horse that stays beautifully bridled and balanced at the slow gait and rack may fall apart at the other gaits. Depending on where the judge is watching, they may catch the best or the worst version of the same horse.

That is why you sometimes see wide spreads like 1-5-X. One judge saw the brilliance. One saw the flat side. One saw a mistake that cost everything. None of those observations are wrong. They are simply incomplete pieces of a bigger picture.

OPINION AND PRIORITIES

We cannot ignore the fact that judging is opinion-based. One judge may prioritize animation and brilliance, another may emphasize manners. Some reward a bold ride, others prefer polish and safety. The rulebook gives a framework, but within that framework, style and perspective matter.

This is not a flaw of the sport. It is part of what makes showing a horse more art than math. Just as one art critic may prefer Picasso and another prefers Monet, one judge may lean toward a horse that oozes expression while another favors the one that never puts a foot out of place. Yes, they are both still following the specifications of the class. That's why three judges balance each other out.

THE REALITY OF SUBJECTIVITY

When you step into a judged sport, you are choosing subjectivity over objectivity. In a race, a stopwatch tells you who won. In equitation or performance classes, it comes down to human judgment. That means outcomes will shift depending on the panel, the day, the competition, and even the arena conditions.

Yes, it can be frustrating, but it is also reality. And the sooner you accept that, the better competitor you will become. Complaining about opinion in a judged sport is like complaining about water in the ocean. It is not going away.

WHAT THE AUDIENCE SEES VS. WHAT JUDGES SEE

Spectators and even trainers on the rail often assume they saw everything that happened. The truth is, they didn't. From the rail, you may be watching one or two horses or a snapshot of the class. A judge is trying to track fifteen. You may think a pass was flawless, but the judge across the ring may have seen a swap of leads, a missed cue, or a break of gait you didn't catch.

This is why cards sometimes baffle the railbirds. The panel is not reacting to the same view you had. They are piecing together a class from very different vantage points, often catching details you didn't see at all.

HOW THE RIGHT HORSE STILL RISES

There is an encouraging part. Over the course of a class, and especially over the course of a show season, the best horses and riders usually find their way to the top. An occasional card split won't stop a consistently superior entry. If your horse belongs at the top, it will win more than it loses, even if one judge sees you differently on a given day.

That is the brilliance of the three-judge system. One opinion cannot dictate the outcome. A panel, averaged together, levels the playing field.

THE TAKEAWAY FOR EXHIBITORS

If one thing from this book sticks with you, I hope it is this: One class, one judge, one panel does not define you or your horse. Even when the cards sting or don't make sense in the moment, remember that it is a snapshot, not the whole story. Your job is not to obsess over every tie. Your job is to keep improving, keep showing, keep loving the process and keep giving the judges more reasons to put you on top.

If you can learn to treat scattered cards as part of the process instead of a personal insult, you will not only last longer in this sport, you will enjoy it more. Because at the end of the day, the right horses and riders earn respect through consistency, not through one perfect card.

FINAL WORD

The next time you hear someone say, *"Those cards were all over the place,"* you can smile to yourself. Because now you know the truth. It is not failure in the system. It is the system doing its job.

4

JUDGING YOUR FRIENDS AND FOES

Judging friends is one of the toughest parts of this sport. It's not openly discussed often, probably because it's messy, emotional, and doesn't come with a clean solution. When someone you love trots into that ring, you're not just evaluating a performance. You're balancing expectations, loyalty, and the real fear of damaging a relationship you care about.

In the same breath, judging people you've had friction with comes with its own brand of pressure. The show ring doesn't ask if you have history. It asks if you're capable of fairness no matter who's number is at the other end of your pen.

If you're going to hold the clipboard, you need to be prepared to judge both friends and foes. And you need to do it with integrity.

THE TIME I ALMOST LOST A FRIEND OVER A JUDGE'S CARD

At one point in my judging career, I found myself in a season that carried both professional significance and personal weight.

I was judging multiple major shows that year, including the World Championship Horse Show.

That season was complicated by the fact that one of my closest friends, someone I had known for more than twenty years, was competing at those same shows.

At an earlier show that year, I placed one of her riders toward the bottom of a very competitive class. It was not a popular decision with her or her barn. I understood why. When you invest deeply in horses, riders, and a program, disappointing results always hurt more when they come from someone you trust.

What escalated the situation was not just the placing itself, but the commentary that followed. At some point, someone made the remark, "With friends like Allison, who needs enemies?" It was said casually, but comments like that have a way of spreading. They get repeated, reshaped, and reinforced until they feel heavier than the original decision ever was.

In the weeks that followed, things were quiet. Not confrontational, just strained. By the time we arrived in Louisville for the World Championship Horse Show, I could sense the tension had not fully cleared. I had the distinct feeling that there was an expectation that I might be harder on her barn this time, perhaps to prove I was not showing favoritism.

That is an uncomfortable place for any friendship to land. Stuck between what actually happened and what people believe happened.

If you were to look at my placings from the show, you would see that I did not judge her barn harshly. I judged the classes. But once a narrative takes hold, facts often struggle to compete with perception. After the World Championship was over, our communication stopped completely. For a time, I genuinely did not know if our friendship was going to recover.

Eventually, it did. We had honest conversations. We acknowledged how much outside voices had influenced the situation. We talked openly about how different it feels to be on opposite sides of the card, especially at a show with stakes as high as the World Championship Horse Show. Today, we are as close as ever.

What that experience taught me was not about blame. It was about perspective. This sport is not just physical. It is also emotional. And when your friend is the one holding the card, disappointment can cut deeper than logic ever will.

That experience taught me a lesson I will never forget. Judging someone you care about does not feel good when the result is not what they hoped for. But rewarding a performance that did not earn it does not feel good either. Your responsibility is not to protect feelings or manage narratives. Your responsibility is to honor the ring.

If the friendship is real, it survives the truth.

THE HARD TRUTH ABOUT PERCEIVED BIAS

Bias exists in this industry. Anyone who tells you otherwise is either inexperienced or unwilling to be honest. That said, bias is not nearly as constant, calculated, or personal as people often believe.

Most perceived bias comes from expectation rather than targeting. Exhibitors often enter into the ring carrying a story about where they believe they should place, based on past wins, money spent, who their trainer is, or how successful the last outing felt. When the ribbon does not match that internal narrative, bias becomes a convenient explanation.

Pressure intensifies this reaction. When the stakes are high, emotions run hot. A placing stops feeling like feedback and starts feeling like a judgment of worth, effort, or legitimacy. Add a familiar judge into the mix, and the assumption quickly becomes, *They know me. They should have understood.*

The reality most exhibitors do not want to hear is, judges are usually not thinking about individuals in the ring nearly as much as people think they are. Judges are managing an entire class, comparing multiple performances, tracking details in real time, and trying to make accurate decisions under pressure. They are not replaying personal history, weighing relationships, or calculating how a ribbon will land emotionally.

This does not mean judges are perfect. It means the ring is not personal, even when it feels deeply personal from the saddle.

When exhibitors assume bias, it often changes how they ride. They can become tentative or overly aggressive. They over-try or ride defensively instead of decisively. That shift in the performance is noticeable, and it frequently affects the outcome of the class.

Not because a judge wanted to send a message, but because the performance itself changed.

The most successful riders, especially at the highest level, understand this distinction. They stop riding against a perceived agenda and start riding the horse underneath them. They trust their preparation, look forward, and allow the performance to speak for itself.

That mindset does not guarantee a ribbon. It does give riders the best possible chance to earn one.

THE OTHER SIDE OF THE COIN

I once had a former client bow out of a show I was judging because she claimed I didn't like her. That was news to me. Truth be told, I haven't thought about her in months, not out of malice, but because I don't carry personal drama into center ring. She assumed my opinion of her would somehow influence her placing. That assumption, while common, is wrong.

If judging friends is uncomfortable, judging people you've had issues with is just as difficult, maybe more. If you're not careful, it's easy to let history cloud your objectivity. You don't even have to dislike them for it to be a problem. Maybe they've badmouthed you. Maybe there's been tension in the warm-up ring. Maybe they've made it clear they don't respect you as a trainer or judge. Whatever the reason, you know there's baggage there and suddenly, they're trotting through the gate. This is the part where your professionalism either holds or cracks.

I've judged people who have openly criticized me, rolled their eyes at me from the rail, or told others I didn't deserve the card I was holding. And I've still placed them first when they earned it.

Why? Because judging isn't about how I feel about you. It's about what I saw in the ring. It's about the performance, the presence, the preparation. You don't have to like me to earn my respect in the show ring. And I don't need to like you to give you a fair shake.

The minute you start letting personal history into your evaluation, you've failed. It's tempting to think someone "deserves to be knocked down a peg." It's tempting to be harsher because "they'd do it to you." However, if you want this industry to rise above pettiness and politics, you've got to rise above it first. Even if no one knows but you. And, in my opinion, that matters more than any placing you write down.

This industry is small. Many of us are friends. Some of us are rivals. A few of us are both. We have coached some of the same students, trained some of the same horses, and definitely competed for the same top titles. But when it's time to judge, those lines have to disappear. Whether it's your best friend or your biggest critic, you owe them the same thing and that is fairness.

I didn't ask for my best friend to be in the ring that day. I didn't ask to judge people who've doubted me, dismissed me, or rooted against me. But I did sign up to be honest.

Any good judge will stand by this, I don't give out ribbons to keep friends. I don't withhold them to settle scores. I give out ribbons to reward performance. The real ones, friends or not, respect that.

5

LET'S TALK ABOUT IT. POLITICS IN JUDGED COMPETITIONS

I hate that this even needs to be a chapter. If you've spent more than a few weekends competing, coaching, or sitting in the stands, you already know that politics exists in judged sports. Is it always at play? No. Is it sometimes a factor? Absolutely. And pretending it doesn't exist doesn't help anyone. While I firmly believe most judges don't want politics to influence their decisions, and many are genuinely working hard to avoid it, the reality is, we're still dealing with human beings. And human beings come with memories, opinions, histories, and unconscious biases.

HOW POLITICS SNEAKS IN (EVEN WHEN JUDGES MEAN WELL)

Sometimes it's as innocent as, a judge is aware of a horse's show record. They know the horse's breeding. They know how much it sold for. They know it's supposed to be the star of the class. Even if they don't intend to give it special treatment, that knowledge can influence where they start mentally when building their card. It's not just the horses. Maybe they recognize the rider's last name, linked to a famous family in the sport. Maybe they know the trainer is a household name. Maybe they associate a certain barn or region with producing winners. None of this means the judge will hand out ribbons unfairly. But it does mean some riders and horses step into the ring with an invisible and unintentional head start and others step in with a chip they'll have to fight to shake off.

The reality of human nature is that recognition can shape perception before the performance even begins. Now, does that mean the horse or rider stays at the top if they don't perform? Not always. Most judges will and should move horses up or down based on what they see. That being said, it is undeniably easier to fall in love with a curated picture that's already been framed for you. It's not fair and it's not how it's supposed to work, but it is human nature. And only the very best of us can completely override it.

DEFENDING THE JUDGES/HUMANS

Before we throw every judge under the bus, let me say this clearly. Politics is less of a factor than most people think. Spectators love to cry about politics when they don't understand the nuances that go into a judge's decision. What looks obvious from the stands is often much more complicated from the center of the ring.

When you're judging, you may see a dropped headset on the lineup pass, a weak step into the corner that cost cadence, tension during a transition, tiny moments, small mistakes, split-second differences that can separate first from fourth. The trained judge's eye catches these details and it is part of the job we were hired to do. The average spectator's eye does not. And when you factor in nerves, angle of view, class size, and horse or rider inconsistencies, it's not hard to understand why sometimes the placings seem surprising to an outside observer. It's just easier, and sometimes more comforting, to blame politics than to face the reality that small, technical differences changed the game.

POLITICS IS RARELY THE WHOLE STORY

Most "political" outcomes are simply the byproduct of:

- A sharper ride
- A stronger moment at the exact right time
- A mistake the rider didn't even feel
- A difference the crowd was not in a position to see
- A judge catching something subtle but significant

When people don't understand the sport at a high level, politics becomes the go-to excuse. High level competitors look deeper.

HUMAN NATURE AND THE POWER OF MEMORY

At the same time, I won't sugarcoat it. When you compete long enough, your name and your reputation stick to you. We cover this topic in other chapters, but if you've built a legacy of strong rides, great sportsmanship, and undeniable performances, congratulations. This can work in your favor. If you've built a history of drama, meltdowns, or sketchy behavior, that can work against you, whether you like it or not. Human memory is sticky. Judges are human. We remember what we remember, even if we're trying not to. You're not just being judged on today. You're being judged on the total impression you've made over time, good, bad, or somewhere in between.

HOW TO BEAT POLITICS: BECOME UNDENIABLE

You can beat politics. You don't beat it by whining. You don't beat it by complaining about how unfair it is. You beat it by becoming so undeniably good that even the most "political" judge has no choice but to place you. Have the cleanest and most commanding presentation. Every detail is polished, turnout, manners, execution. The sharpest mindset. Calm, prepared, competitive without desperation. The hardest worker. Leaving no doubt that you've earned every ounce of your success. The most resilient presence.

Win or lose, you look like a winner every time you enter the ring. You don't just deserve to win, you make it obvious. Obvious even to a judge who didn't want to notice you. Obvious even to a crowd full of skeptics. And once you've made it obvious, the politics lose their power.

ALWAYS A BRIDESMAID

Being "always a bridesmaid" in the show horse world means you're consistently near the top. You have a great horse, strong rides, and you're clearly in the running. But for some reason, you keep ending up second. You're respected, but not yet the one they expect to call out first. You have the horse, the rider, the training, and the results. You just don't have the political edge or the timing. That's the sad truth. In classes where it's close, judges often default to the one who has won before. Familiar names can bring a sense of confidence to a judging panel.

When all the pieces are strong across the board, that past performance record can give someone the slight edge. It doesn't mean you're not worthy, it just means you're still building the kind of presence that wins the class on reputation as well as performance. You might be clean, correct, and polished, but you're not tipping the scale. You haven't built enough buzz. Maybe your name hasn't been called enough times for the entire panel to feel like it is easy putting you on top.

You're not being overlooked, but you're also not the first choice. Not yet. So why does it keep happening? For starters, you might be playing it too safe. You're consistent, but not commanding. Clean rides are great, but they don't always create the kind of presence that wins the class. Sometimes, judges reward boldness over controlled perfection, especially when everything else is equal. If you're showing like you're trying to survive the class instead of own it, that energy shows up in your performance.

Another possibility is that you're in the wrong division. Maybe your horse can hold its own, but it's not the ideal fit. You've chosen the division that excites you instead of the one that sets your horse up to shine. Judges can tell when a horse is being forced to play a part instead of starring in its natural role.

It is also possible you simply haven't built the momentum yet. This is a sport where success builds on itself. When it's tight, judges go with the name they've already written down in the past. If you're newer to the level, or going up against riders who've won repeatedly, you're not just competing with horses, you're competing with history.

Sometimes the only thing missing is that extra edge of memorability. You're not forgettable, but you're not unforgettable either. You're doing everything right, but you haven't crossed the threshold where the panel sees you as the obvious winner. Getting past this stage takes intentional work. First, change your intent. Stop riding like you're trying to avoid a mistake. Ride like you belong in the winner's circle. Judges feel that shift. Next, audit your entire presentation. From your outfit to your entrance to your energy, are you presenting a complete, undeniable package or just hoping to be noticed? Then, shift the story. Start promoting your program. Celebrate the progress. Talk up your horse. Talk like a winner and ride like one. If people expect you to win, eventually the judges will too. Create energy around you. A rider with buzz gets watched more closely. And when the class is tight, energy often tips the scale.

Finally, stay in it. The breakthrough usually comes after the longest plateau. Keep showing up with polish, professionalism, and presence until you become impossible to ignore. If you keep landing second, it means you're close. And close is where all the legends start.

Being "always a bridesmaid" is rarely about talent. It's about energy, presence and intent. You don't go from second to first by riding more safely. You go from second to first by riding braver. Judges reward riders who ride like they expect to win, not riders hoping not to blow it.

If you're stuck in second, the problem isn't your skill. The problem is your belief. Shift the belief, and the ride follows.

THE POWER OF CONSISTENCY: HOW TO MAKE POLITICS IRRELEVANT

Something else I can promise you is that consistently putting in top rides at big shows will absolutely help you become undeniable. Even if you don't win right away, you'll start to create buzz around you and your horse. People will talk. They'll say how great your ride was, whether you were tied first, fifth, or not called out at all. Do that regularly, ride like a champion over and over again, and eventually, you'll find a judge who will reward it. It only takes one. That's my theory, and I've seen it proven over and over again.

It only takes one judge to tie you first over the reigning World Champion, the "million-dollar horse," or the World Grand Champion trainer. Once one judge does it, it gives the others permission to do it too. You just have to be ready for it. You have to keep showing up, keep being undeniable, and keep believing that your breakthrough is coming. It only takes one. And if you stay ready, one day you'll hear your name announced as the unanimous World Champion.

REMEMBER: IT'S AN OPINION, NOT A FORMULA

A common theme in this book is that judges are human and we tend to forget this fact. They have different backgrounds, experiences, and preferences, just like anyone else. One judge might value a breathtaking front end above all else. Another might zero in on timing, or correctness, or overall picture. Some fall in love with a beautiful head. Others care more about a balanced, correct headset or how the horse uses its hind end. And of course, all of us love the rare horse who has it ALL. Just like people have different favorite colors, they also have different ideas of what the "best" five-gaited horse in America looks like.

Yes, there are specifications in the rulebook that a judge is supposed to follow. But the interpretation of those specs is still up to the individual. What might be a fatal flaw to one judge, a step or two on the wrong lead, a crooked stop, a couple bounces before a flat walk, might be something another judge forgives, depending on how severe it was, how it happened, and what else was going on in the class.

One judge might be hyper-focused on a minor bobble. Another might not see it as enough to outweigh a horse's overall quality or presence. As exhibitors, trainers, instructors, and riders, we have to take this into account or we'll find ourselves constantly disenchanted with the sport. And we all spend too much time, energy, and heart to feel disappointed all the time. This is a judged sport. When you trot through that in-gate, you're knowingly and willingly signing up for someone's opinion on that particular day. That's not a flaw in the system, it is the system.

POLITICS MAY EXIST, BUT EXCELLENCE STILL WINS

Judged competitions will never be perfect. Human beings will always have human biases. Politics will show up sometimes where it doesn't belong. But excellence has a power politics can't completely defeat. Excellence commands attention. It silences doubts. It rises over time, over setbacks, over noise. And those who stay committed to becoming truly, undeniably great? They still win. Maybe not every class. Maybe not every show. Maybe not in the timeline they wished for, but nonetheless, they do win in the end. Because in the long game, the only game that really matters, the cream always rises.

The ones who refused to blame politics...the ones who kept sharpening, kept improving, kept believing...they are the ones who end up leading the sport. Don't waste your energy wishing the system was fairer. Use that energy to become the kind of competitor no system can ignore. You don't need perfect judging to build a legendary career. You just need to become undeniable.

6

THIS IS NOT A FASHION SHOW (THOUGH I LOVE THE GOWNS)

Allison, judging the World Championship Horse Show in 2018. Photo by Howard Schatzberg.

I was thirty-eight years old when I was asked to judge the World's Championship Horse Show. It was a moment I had been quietly preparing for since I was a little girl sitting in the balcony seats at Freedom Hall. I was barely old enough to fully understand what I was watching, but I vividly remember Skywatch and Michele McFarlane winning the World Grand Championship in 1988. Michele becoming the first woman to win the coveted title. It remains one of the most exciting and defining moments in horse show history, and it left a permanent mark on me.

Like many kids, I dreamed of showing at Louisville. That dream, however, came true early in my life. Judging it, on the other hand, came along much later.

Back then, there were not many women judging the World's Championship Horse Show. When they were hired, they often judged equitation classes, and as an aspiring equitation rider, I watched those classes closely. Naturally, I ended up watching the judges as well. I paid attention to how they stood, how they carried themselves, and yes, what they wore. I have always loved clothes and the way an outfit can match a moment. Seeing strong, respected women standing confidently in center ring on the green shavings mattered to me. It made the future feel possible.

As more women began judging all divisions at Louisville, I became obsessed with the evening gowns. Judges like Melissa and Melinda Moore, Lisa Waller, and others turned Freedom Hall into something that felt even more electric than normal. A runway with purpose.

Judging is not a fashion show. I know that. But showing up dressed thoughtfully and with professionalism is part of respecting the sanctity of our sport. It signals that you understand the magnitude of the moment and the responsibility that comes with it.

I take judging seriously. I care deeply about the weight of

my decisions. Those decisions affect careers, horse values, breeding programs, and lifelong dreams. So no, it was never about the gowns (though admittedly, I love an excuse to wear an evening gown). It was about honoring the institution.

GETTING THE CALL

Not everyone who earns a judge's card aspires to judge Louisville. I did. From the moment I got my card, that was the goal. I did not say it out loud to anyone except my mom. I think I was embarrassed to admit something that ambitious.

Why would anyone want an inexperienced, relatively unknown trainer from Oregon to judge the greatest horse show in the world? My mom, thankfully, did not agree.

In February of 2017, Buddy Waggoner was floating teeth at our barn. My mom told him that judging Louisville was my goal. I had never planned to tell anyone. Which probably meant I never would have reached it.

Before Buddy left, he asked me if I was serious about judging Louisville. "Of course," I said, trying not to sound like a six-year-old who had just been handed the keys to Freedom Hall. "Give it a year," he replied.

I did not think much about it after that. Then, in February of 2018, my phone rang. The caller ID read Scarlet Mattson, the show manager of the World Championship Horse Show. I assumed she was calling to ask me to judge another one of her shows. Instead, she said, "Do you want to judge Louisville?"

Trying to sound calm and professional, I replied, "I would be honored. Let me make sure my dad is okay not showing at Louisville this year."

I hung up and immediately told my dad that we were absolutely not showing at Louisville because I was judging it. I called Scarlet back the next day and accepted.

THE WEIGHT OF THE DECISION

What many people do not realize is that accepting a judging job at Louisville is not just an honor. It is a business decision. A complicated one.

Judging the World's Championship Horse Show can cost a trainer income. Clients may move their horses to another trainer months in advance so they can be eligible to compete in front of you. Clients with world-level goals generally do not want to skip a year. It is not a small ask to potentially lose clients, income and opportunities.

There is also the personal side. You will judge friends, former clients, former situationships. People who know you well enough to expect something, whether they admit it or not.

There is pressure from every direction. And yes, for the women judging the show, there is also the reality that eight, plus an extra or two in case of emergency, evening gowns do not magically appear in your closet without significant effort or expense.

The weight is real. Financially. Emotionally. Professionally. Despite all of it, I was probably the most excited person to ever be asked to judge on the green shavings. I had been preparing for this moment since I was eight years old.

By the end of February, my gowns were chosen. By April, daytime outfits were planned. My exercise, health, and beauty routines went into full focus. It felt like preparing for a wedding, but with significantly more pressure and fewer champagne toasts.

THE CRASH BEFORE THE DREAM

The day before the show, on my way to pick up my Thursday night gown from the seamstress, I was in a serious car accident.

No one has ever accused me of being an exceptional driver, but I promise this one was not my fault.

I was physically fine, but I spent hours in the emergency room panicking because my gowns were in the now-totaled rental car, possibly being towed to a random junkyard.

Fortunately for me, Byron Day answered my call that night and became my hero. Unfortunately for him, most everyone else I knew in the area was already in Louisville by then, so he was my one and only savior. He picked me up from Woodford County Hospital, drove me to wherever the car had been taken, and helped me rescue my dresses. We secured a new rental car, and I finally arrived at the Crowne Plaza well after midnight.

So much for quiet preparation.

THE EMOTIONAL REALITY OF JUDGING LOUISVILLE

What I want people to understand is that the highs and lows of this sport do not belong only to the competitors. Judges feel them too. The emotions I experienced over eight days rivaled how I feel when I am actually showing there.

I felt nerves and excitement walking down the ramp for the first Saturday night performance. Mild disappointment when I realized I was not judging until the third class. Anxiety the first time I stepped out of the judge's stand with my card in hand.

Panic during the first morning of qualifiers when four riders would regularly come at me abreast in identical suits on chestnut horses and I had to make split-second decisions.

Pride when one of my closest friends earned her first Freedom Hall ribbon after thirty years of trying.

Sadness when that same year, another close friend believed I had placed her rider unfairly.

A deep sense of responsibility judging the many qualifying classes, realizing that first through eighth all mattered. At this level, fewer than half the class earns the right to come back. That reality never left my mind.

I was in awe judging future legends as young horses and ponies, such as Beauty Marc, The Crowd Went Nuts, Callaway's Ivanka, Starlette and more. Horses that would go on to define their divisions.

Pure exhaustion by Wednesday night after judging hundreds and hundreds of horses in their qualifiers for the previous four days.

And then renewed excitement from Thursday night through Saturday, knowing I would be watching the very best our sport has to offer. Believe me when I tell you, not having a session on Thursday morning is not just for the trainers to have a break. The judges need the reset too.

I will never forget what one of my fellow judges, Johnny Jones, said to me when I arrived at the show to judge on Thursday night. As we were walking into Freedom Hall, he turned to me and said, "It's just a three-day horse show now."

I remember looking at him in confusion. I understood how many days were left on the schedule, but I did not yet understand why it mattered.

He went on to explain, "It's like judging any other show now. Except it's three days of judging the best horses in the world. And that's easy."

That comment stayed with me. Not because the responsibility disappears, but because by that point so much has already been revealed. The pace has settled. The distractions have quieted. The week has done its work. When everything else has been filtered out, the job becomes simple. You simply get to judge quality against quality and that is Louisville at its most distilled.

WOULD I DO IT AGAIN?

The answer depends on when you asked me. After the first three days of the show, the answer would have been absolutely not. I was exhausted. My brain was full. I could tell a friend was upset with me. And I knew it was only going to get harder.

On the Sunday after the show was over, maybe. By then, many people had already texted or called to thank me for taking the time to judge, for giving everyone a fair look, and of course to compliment my outfits. Those messages meant more to me than people probably realized, and I am still grateful to those who reached out.

A month after the show, maybe not. By then, you become painfully aware of who is mad at you, who thinks you wronged them, and who will "never show under you again." At that point, the idea of being judged as the judge anytime soon does not sound particularly appealing.

A year later, yes. By then, the negative emotions had faded, the perspective had returned, and I was ready to romanticize the idea again. I still want to do it again. And again. And again.

Right now, my training career does not allow me to skip a year at the World's Championship Horse Show. Coming from the West Coast is a commitment, and when clients invest in world-level goals, I do not want them to miss opportunities. Truthfully, I do not want to miss them either.

But when my life shifts, I will absolutely do everything I can to get back in the center ring at Freedom Hall. I have already started picking out my gowns.

Allison and her husband, Marc Hevern on "Stake Night" in 2018 while judging the World Championship Horse Show. Photo by Howard Schatzberg.

7

THE WINNER'S MINDSET

"Every class is winnable until the judge's cards are turned in. I don't care what horse I'm on, who else is in the class, or what the odds look like from the rail. I ride like it is mine to lose, because sometimes that belief is the very thing that tips the scale in my favor."

In the high stakes world of competitive riding, belief is not a cute attitude. It is your edge. The certainty that you can win, no matter the circumstances, is what separates the rider who makes an impression from the one who blends into the crowd. The show ring tests more than your skill. It tests how long you are willing to bet on yourself, even when the class starts to unravel. If you do not believe you can win, you hand the advantage to someone else before the first pass even happens.

THE POWER OF BELIEF

When you trot through the gate, the judge is rooting for you. Yes, you. No matter what barn you ride with or how long you have been showing, our job is to find a winner. I would love nothing more than for every rider to show up and make our decisions difficult because you all look like winners. Judges want that moment of clarity when someone rides with so much conviction and presence that the choice becomes obvious.

I have watched countless classes come down to two or three riders who were nearly equal in turnout, talent and horsepower. In the end, what separated them was their mindsets. The winner was usually the one who held it together when the pressure hit, who kept showing like there was still something to gain. The ones who fade, doubt, or coast as soon as a mistake shows up might make my job easier, but they do not make the victory pass.

Belief is not pretending to be perfect. It is staying mentally in the game after something goes wrong. Judges know when a rider is still fighting for it and we know when they have checked out. Your belief in yourself, your ride and your horse; and your drive to get to the winner's circle is what keeps us watching you.

RIDING THROUGH MISTAKES

Perfection is a myth in this sport. Horses are unpredictable. Nerves hit and mistakes happen, sometimes in the first thirty seconds. But the class is not over until I turn in my card. I have given ribbons to riders who had an early bobble but regrouped and rode their hearts out for the rest of the class. How you recover is everything. The second mistake riders make is letting their confidence slip. Shoulders drop, focus scatters, posture collapses, and the connection with the horse unravels. That is the moment the class is truly lost.

The truth is most people can ride well when everything goes right. That does not impress judges. That is expected. What separates serious competitors from average ones is the ability to recover quickly, adjust intelligently, and move forward without emotional fallout when something goes wrong.

Mistakes are not always what cost you the class. Emotional reactions do. Judges do not expect perfection. We expect composure. When a mistake happens, we immediately watch what comes next. Does the rider panic or reset? Do they tighten and micromanage, or do they rebalance and ride on? Do they dwell on the error, or do they stay present and ride the class that is still in front of them?

The best riders treat a mistake as a data point, not a verdict. They fix what can be fixed, let go of what cannot, and keep riding with purpose. Their body language stays confident. Their focus stays forward. Their horse stays supported instead of blamed. That ability to stay mentally upright after a stumble is one of the most valuable skills a rider can develop, and it cannot be faked.

There is only one way to learn it. You have to keep getting on. You have to keep showing. You have to keep putting yourself in situations where the pressure is real.

You do not build recovery skills in perfect rides. You build them by riding through imperfection over and over again until adjusting becomes automatic. Until your instinct is to sit up, breathe, and keep riding instead of spiraling.

Riders who master this skill look unshakeable in the ring. They are not flawless. They are resilient. And resilience wins far more classes than sporadic and unpredictable perfection ever will.

THE DAY I FELL OFF AND STILL WON

One of my most important lessons came when I was fifteen, riding a green horse in a big equitation class. Another rider's horse ran into mine at the canter, and I hit the ground before I fully understood what had happened. I was stunned and humiliated. I was certain the class was over. But when I got back on, I made a conscious decision. I rode like the blue ribbon was still possible.

I sat up taller. I rode with intention. I stopped replaying the fall and started riding the class that was still happening. Every stride mattered. Every moment counted. And somehow, though in hindsight not somehow at all, I won.

Later that night, the judge saw me in the hotel lobby. He stopped me and said, "You know, you didn't need to worry. I saw what happened, and I saw how you handled it."

That moment has stayed with me my entire career. You cannot always control what goes wrong in the ring. Horses are animals. Situations change. Accidents happen. What judges care about, and what separates real competitors from everyone else, is what you do next.

How you respond tells us everything.

BODY LANGUAGE THAT WINS

One of the key things that separates winners from everyone else is body language. You do not need to be the loudest or boldest rider in the arena. You simply need to train your body to reflect your belief. Judges see everything. Posture, tension, hesitation, confidence, quitting energy, and the tiny shift in expression that says a rider thinks they are already out of the running.

What winning body language looks like:

- **Sit up and ride like you're proud of yourself.** Even if you are nervous, claim your space in the saddle. Show everyone that you belong there.
- **Stay relaxed but anchored.** Create the balance between strength and suppleness. Your horse feels it and the judge sees it.

- **Keep your eyes in the game.** Forward, soft focus. No staring at your hands or scanning the arena in panic.
- **Breathe with intention.** Deep, steady breathing before you go in and throughout the class. Your horse will mirror you.
- **Wear your game face.** Confidence or calm determination. Your expression speaks long before your skills do.
- **Finish strong.** Ride like the class is still winnable until you line up.

THE COMPETITIVE EDGE

You do not know what the judge has seen. The horse that looks flawless from the stands may have spooked, swapped leads, hesitated, or blown a transition directly in front of me. The rider you think is winning may already be off my card. That is exactly why you never assume you are out.

Riders lose more classes in their own head than they ever lose on paper. One mistake happens and they mentally check out. The ride softens, the presence fades and they stop riding like they belong at the top of the line. And that, not the mistake, is what costs them.

The class is not over until the ribbons are handed out. Period. Judges reward riders who stay in the fight. Riders who keep riding with purpose. Riders who do not ask the judge to excuse them by shrinking after a mistake. When everyone else is riding defensively, the competitor who keeps showing up, stride after stride, becomes impossible to ignore.

More classes than people realize are not won by perfection. They are won by refusal, the refusal to quit, the refusal to assume and the refusal to stop riding.

That is the competitive edge.

THE "ALMOST" RIDER

Every trainer and every judge knows the "almost" rider. Always solid. Always consistent. Always safe. And almost never on top. These riders have the skill, the position, and the discipline to be competitive, but they lack the spark that makes a judge sit up and take notice.

I have coached riders like this **over the years**. The hardest part is not the riding, it is the awareness. Most "almost" riders do not realize this is how they are showing. And if you cannot see it, you cannot fix it. That is what makes this phase so difficult to coach someone through.

Here is the good news. This is not a permanent label. Once a rider is willing to recognize it and take responsibility for changing it, the shift can happen. Awareness comes first. Intention follows. And with the right guidance, "almost" can become competitive, then credible, and eventually, winning.

How to break out of the "almost" trap:

- **Be memorable.** Correct is not enough. Take a calculated risk. Add intention to your transitions. Ride with a presence that makes me look twice.
- **Get honest feedback.** Ask a judge or experienced trainer to evaluate you from the center ring perspective, not as a cheerleader but as a critic. You will learn far more from the truth than from polite encouragement.

Winning starts long before the lineup. It begins with the way you think, the way you prepare, and the way you show up when things go wrong. The riders who rise to the top are not always those who have the perfect horses or flawless passes. They are the ones who refuse to shrink, who stay mentally in the fight, and who ride every stride like it matters. If you build that mindset, you give yourself a chance to win every time you step into the ring and that is the kind of rider judges never forget.

YOU'RE NOT TOO LATE. BUT YOU DO HAVE TO ACT LIKE YOU'RE ON TIME

Tina Sutter & CH Undulata's High Society winning a World Championship at ages 67 and 17, respectively. Proof its never too late to chase your dreams.

One of the great advantages of this sport is longevity. You are not racing a clock that suddenly runs out. You can build skill, confidence, and success over decades if you choose to. What holds most people back is not age or timing, but hesitation. Waiting to feel ready. Waiting for the perfect horse, the perfect season, the perfect confidence level. That moment rarely comes on its own.

Professionals are not immune to this mindset either. Even at the top levels, it is easy to feel behind or to believe you should already be further along than you are. In fact, I have had those thoughts myself. But when you step back and look honestly at the careers of many of the most successful riders and trainers, a clear pattern emerges. Their strongest years often come later than expected. This sport rewards persistence. It rewards consistency. It rewards the people who keep showing up, refining their skills, and staying in the game long enough for everything to finally click.

If you want proof that it is not too late, look at who lasts. The riders and trainers who rise to the top are not always the youngest or the flashiest. They are the ones who stay consistent, who keep learning, and who refuse to opt out mentally when progress feels slower than expected. This sport rewards long games, not quick wins.

YOUR AGE DOES NOT DISQUALIFY YOU. YOUR EXCUSES DO.

If you are still riding, you are still rising. This is not your last chance. It is your next move.

If you believe you are behind, stop measuring yourself against imaginary timelines and start measuring actions. Are you riding with purpose, or just going through the motions? Are you seeking feedback from people who will actually tell you the truth? Are you watching classes, studying results, and learning how the game is really played? Those habits matter far more than how long you have been in the saddle.

If fitness feels like a limitation, address it directly. You do not need to be twenty years old, but you do need to be prepared. Strength, balance, stamina, and recovery are trainable at any age. Treat them like part of your riding program, not an optional add-on. If confidence is the issue, build it the same way you build skill: through repetition, preparation, and putting yourself in situations that stretch you slightly beyond comfort.

Most importantly, stop giving yourself exit language. Phrases like last chance, too old, or I should have done this sooner quietly lower your standards and expectations. Replace them with forward-focused questions. What would it look like to take this season seriously? What would change if I trained like someone who expects to improve? What am I willing to commit to over the next six months, not someday, but now?

You are not late. But momentum only shows up when effort does. Show up with clarity. Show up prepared. Show up as if progress is still expected, because it is. In this sport, timing is not about age. It is about action.

Ring Reset

10 Things That Require Zero Talent

These are habits that require no talent, no special horse, and no luck, yet they are some of the fastest ways to look prepared, confident, and competitive in the show ring.

1. Trotting In With Intent
You don't need talent to show up like you mean it.
Own the ring.

2. Listening Like It Matters
Great riders hear what's said the first time. Then apply it.

3. Staying Present Under Pressure
Zoning out or spiraling helps no one. Be where your horse is.

4. Soft in the Face, Firm in the Core
Feel starts with your body language.

5. Fixing It Now, Not Later
Don't wait for perfect timing or a fresh start. Try to fix something in the moment.

6. Using Your Turns Like a Pro
A thinking rider uses the whole arena to their advantage.

7. Practicing the Easy Stuff Like It's Hard
Because it is when the pressure's on.

8. Staying Open, Not Defensive
You're not being corrected because you're bad. You're being coached because you're capable.

9. Loving the Work More Than the Applause
Ribbons don't make riders. Rides do.

10. Making the Horse Feel Like a Genius
That's not talent. That's leadership.

Save this page and return to it before your class, or whenever you need to reset and refocus.

8

BELIEF IS A MUSCLE

The belief that you can win is not a one-time decision. It is a muscle, and like any muscle, it gets stronger with repetition and weaker with neglect. Confidence is something you choose over and over again, especially on the days it feels furthest from reach. Training your mind is as much a part of this sport as training your horse. It requires consistency, intention, and a long-game perspective.

One of the simplest ways to strengthen that mental muscle is to build pre-class rituals that help to ground you. A short phrase quietly repeated as you trot in can flip your nervous system into readiness. It can be something as simple as "I'm ready," "Ride with purpose," or "I belong here." Say it under your breath. Say it in your mind. Say it until your body responds. These cues work not because they are poetic, but because repetition conditions your brain to match the energy you want to bring into the ring. Belief isn't just something you rehearse the night before, it has to live in your body, your decisions, and the way you ride.

Visualization is another tool used by serious competitors. Spend five minutes the night before a show picturing your best entrance, your boldest pass, and your number being called to the winner's circle. Let yourself feel that moment. Treat it like it already happened. Your mind will follow the patterns you train it to follow. Visualization prepares your body to execute under pressure because you have already lived the moment internally.

THE DISCIPLINE OF ALREADY WINNING

Bob Proctor and Allison's husband, Marc Hevern on stage at personal development seminar

While the outcome of a class is never fully in your control, your mindset always is, and it determines how you show up. When that mindset shifts from hoping to executing, you enter the ring in a different category altogether.

I learned this concept firsthand when I was coached by world-renowned personal development coach Bob Proctor. We were discussing the idea of riding as if you had already won the class. Not wishing nor pretending, but operating as if the outcome was already secured.

As a horse trainer, my immediate reaction was skepticism. Horses have their own minds, their own reactions, and their own limits. You cannot sit one down and explain that today is the day they take their victory pass, although I have absolutely tried.

So I asked the obvious question. If I genuinely believe I

have already won and ride every step as if I am already on the victory pass, what about the horse? How do I get the horse to believe they've already won?

Of course, he didn't hesitate. He explained that when you are truly operating at the level of a winner, when your thoughts, emotions, body language, and expectations are aligned, everything around you responds accordingly. Judges, competitors, situations, and yes, animals. Certainty, calm authority, and confidence without tension are contagious.

That answer challenged me. I spend every day of my life training horses, and I know results come from preparation, repetition, and discipline, not daydreaming. The more I thought about it, the more it made sense.

Horses are not responding to your goals. They are responding to your state. They read posture before pressure. Breath before aids. Purpose before instruction.

A rider who is hoping reads as tight. A rider who is unsure reads as hesitant. A rider who is trying too hard to win reads as forceful. A rider who expects to execute the win moves differently.

When your mind is calm and resolved, your body follows. Timing improves. Aids become clearer. Your hands stop asking unnecessary questions. The horse receives clarity instead of conflict.

That is what being on the same vibration actually means. It is not magic. Your job is to show up so prepared, so grounded, and so certain that the horse has no reason to question what is being asked.

When your internal conversation changes from "I hope this goes well" to "I know how this ride feels," the ride becomes more efficient, more confident, and more deliberate.

That is when execution replaces hope. And that is when winning becomes familiar instead of feeling like you got lucky.

THE WORK CONTINUES

Erin Cummings, Sandy Gallagher and Allison Deardorff celebrating Sandy's first World Championship. Photo by Julie Anne Broder.

"Visualization isn't fantasy, it's mental rehearsal for success. When you ride the class in your mind with clarity and certainty, you prepare your body and your horse to do the same."

-Sandy Gallagher

That same perspective was reinforced for me through my friendship with Sandy Gallagher, Bob's longtime business partner and the person closest to his work. Sandy and I shared her first and my first professional World Championship together, an experience that gave real-world context to the principles Bob taught. Seeing those ideas applied under pressure helped clarify how belief functions in practice, not as optimism, but as commitment.

Sandy's approach mirrors what Bob emphasized that outcomes are shaped well before they are announced. Preparation, expectation, and execution are aligned long before a rider enters the ring. Being around that mindset sharpened my understanding of visualization as something grounded and disciplined rather than abstract.

Part of riding like a winner is knowing how to recover like one. A missed lead or bobble doesn't define your ride, your recovery does. Winners don't spiral, they re-center. That presence is part of what horses trust.

When belief is settled early and reinforced through preparation, everything else becomes quieter. The horse feels it. The ride feels different. And the focus shifts from hoping for a result to allowing it to unfold.

THE IDENTITY TRAP

Before we go any further into strategy, ringside politics, or performance, we have to address the mental landmine that quietly derails more riders than anything happening inside the ring. This is the point where the conversation shifts from mechanics to mindset. If your identity is tangled up in your results, nothing else in this book will land the way it should. You cannot ride like a winner while using the sport to prove something about who you are.

In many cases, riders do not just want to win. They want winning to validate something inside of them. That is where the danger lies. The more time, money, and emotion you invest, the easier it is to believe that your last ribbon reflects your worth. When you win, you feel enough. When you do not, you feel like you fell short. This thinking does not make you competitive. It makes you fragile and anxious.

I have watched incredibly capable riders mentally collapse because one judge's opinion did not match their own expectations. Beautiful rides fall apart backstage because the rider's internal dialogue becomes toxic: "Everyone thinks I failed," or "Why do I bother?" Let me be clear. Wanting to win is healthy.

Needing to win to feel worthy is not. Your value has never been nor will it ever be determined by a judge's card.

IDENTITY ANCHORS

The riders who stay grounded and rise consistently do not renegotiate their identity after every placing. Instead, they anchor it. Identity anchors are small, personal reminders you choose ahead of time that keep your confidence stable when nerves or doubt show up. Some riders carry a token in their pocket, touch a bracelet before trotting in, read a note tucked into their coat, or repeat a private sentence that brings them back to who they are.

Your anchor might be a phrase like "Ride for progress, not perfection," or "This is one class, not my whole identity." It could be a reminder of someone who believed in you, a quiet breath that signals readiness, or a personal "why" statement you revisit before you show. Anchors are not soft sentiments. They are psychological stability points that prevent you from handing your self-worth over to the person holding the clipboard standing in the middle of the arena. They protect your ambition by keeping it focused on the controlables, your preparation, your presence, and your partnership with your horse.

Judges can feel the steadiness of a rider who is anchored in something deeper than today's outcome. Horses feel it too. That steadiness becomes a competitive advantage, because it shows up as composure when others crack.

WHY YOUR HORSE MATTERS

At the center of all this pressure, ambition, and mindset work is a horse. An animal who meets you where you are every ride and can mirror your internal state back to you. Some of the most meaningful moments in this sport never happen when your name is called. They happen quietly, behind the scenes, when your horse finally flat walks with softness, or when you feel your hands and body communicate in a way they never have before. They happen when you step off after a tough ride and know your horse tried hard and you stayed mentally present for them.

Those moments never end up on a trophy shelf, but they shape you more than any ribbon ever will. A ribbon may validate you for a night. A true partnership with your horse can carry you through a lifetime of riding.

CHASING THE RIGHT THINGS

Show like you are there to win. Practice, prepare, and take pride in how you present yourself. However, when the only thing you chase is a specific ribbon, your riding and your horse suffer. Your decisions get reactive and anxiety replaces clarity.

Ribbons are outcomes and outcomes are unstable. When you chase growth, connection, and mastery, you ride from a place that is far more powerful. You stay present, you adapt and you ride the horse you have in that moment instead of forcing the ride you imagined. That internal stability cannot be taken away by one judge, one card, or one result.

This is not about lowering expectations. It is about raising your foundation. Riders who anchor themselves in development rather than validation show up differently. Their timing is quieter. Their focus is sharper. Their mistakes are smaller and their recoveries faster. They are not emotionally swinging with every stride because their confidence is not dependent on immediate approval.

The riders who look calm, confident, and dangerous in a competitive class understand this distinction. They are prepared to win, but not attached to the outcome. They ride from grounded identity, not desperation and this is the reason they are always a threat.

WHEN CONFIDENCE BECOMES UNSHAKABLE

We have established that your worth has never and never should come from a judge's opinion, and the most successful riders know this. When your identity is rooted in purpose, preparation, and partnership rather than outcomes, your confidence becomes durable. You enter the ring already centered, and from a judge's perspective, that presence is almost impossible to ignore. This sport rewards riders who stay composed when others panic, who breathe when others freeze, and who continue to show up even after things go wrong.

Most riders lose a class because they mentally quit long before the judge stops watching. Do not be that rider. Be the competitor who stays in it until the very last stride. Be the rider who finishes strong and gives the judge something to remember. Many classes are won not by the most expensive horse or the biggest barn, but by the rider who never stopped believing the class was winnable.

Cultivating a winner's mindset is not optional. It is one of the strongest competitive advantages you can develop, and it is entirely within your control. When you train your thoughts with the same discipline you train your horse, you become more resilient, more present, and more capable under pressure. You become the rider who does not fold after mistakes, who stays grounded from the first pass to the lineup, and who brings purpose rather than panic into every class. That is the kind of presence judges reward, horses trust, and competitors notice.

Let this chapter be your reminder that belief is built, not inherited. Build it daily, protect it fiercely, and ride like someone who knows they deserve to be in that ring.

9
WE CAN'T ALL BE JORDAN (OR TOM MOORE) AND THAT'S OK

Tom Moore & WGC CH Yorktown winning the Five Gaited World Grand Championship in 1970. Photo by Sargent.

One of the often unspoken challenges riders face as they advance in this sport is reconciling ambition with reality. We are encouraged to want more, to push harder, and to aim higher, and rightly so. However, ambition without context can become corrosive. When riders believe that wanting success requires chasing a specific version of it, comparison takes over. Progress begins to feel insufficient, not because effort is lacking, but because expectations have been borrowed rather than built. This chapter exists to reset that narrative.

UNDERSTANDING LIMITS WITHOUT LOSING DRIVE

In another chapter, I mention my very short-lived basketball career as an example of when work ethic can make up for less talent. However, there's another factor that matters just as much: even without the knee surgery, I was never headed to the WNBA, no matter how much I practiced. That realization, as unglamorous as it was, taught me something I still use today. Believe me, I am not saying this to discourage anyone. I want to be crystal clear about that. I am not telling you to lower your goals or disarm your aspirations because I said you might not become the next Tom Moore of the Saddlebred world. You still need to aim for the stars. Reach for them. Grab them. Hang on. That part is non-negotiable regardless of how good you can become.

What is important to understand is that your equestrian journey may look different than your barn mate's. Or the rider who seems to win everything. Or the trainer whose name is already etched into the history books. We can't all be Michael Jordan. And that does not make the rest of us irrelevant.

One of the most misunderstood things about this sport is the assumption that everyone in the ring is chasing the same outcome. The reality is, they aren't. From the rail, it looks uniform. Same arena. Same judges. Same class. Same ribbons waiting at the end. However, the reasons riders are there could not be more different. Some are chasing a championship. Some are chasing consistency. Some are proving something to themselves. Some are giving a young horse experience. Some are rebuilding confidence after a bad season, a bad fall, or a bad year. Everyone's path is valid.

This sport is rare because everyone can participate and everyone can compete. We can show in the same ring, under the same judges, in the same class, with wildly different skills, goals, resources, bodies, and timelines, and all belong there. That is not a flaw in the system. That is the beauty of it.

The mistake riders make is assuming that because the ring is shared, the journey should be identical. This is where frustration creeps in. When ambition is filtered through comparison instead of context, even progress can feel like failure. Riders start measuring themselves against careers, resources, or timelines that were never theirs to begin with.

WHERE THIS LESSON FINALLY CLICKED FOR ME

The moment this idea really crystallized for me did not happen while judging or showing at a major competition. In fact, it happened during a regular riding lesson.

I was teaching a client who is also a close friend. She is a naturally good rider and she works very hard. We were working on something specific and fairly advanced with her horse. It was a skill that can elevate a ride, but it was not essential to their overall success as a team. She was struggling to grasp the concept and having an even harder time executing it consistently. From my perspective, this was not a reflection of her talent or effort. It was simply an area that was likely never going to be her strongest, and I was completely comfortable with that.

Trying to ease her frustration, I said something I believed was reassuring. I told her not to worry about it and that we cannot all ride like Tom Moore, and that that was okay.

To put that statement into proper context, it would be an oversight not to acknowledge who Tom Moore was and why his name carries so much weight in this industry. He is arguably the "Jordan" of the Saddlebred world, and widely regarded as one of the greatest and most influential horsemen the industry has ever known. His impact extended far beyond winning. He shaped the modern industry as a trainer, elevated the breed as a showman, and helped establish the professional structure that still governs it today. What truly set him apart was his extraordinary feel for a horse, his ability to think with the horse rather than impose himself upon it, and his unmatched composure under pressure. When it mattered most, he was at his best. Riders like that are rare. They redefine what excellence looks like, much like Micheal Jordan or Tiger Woods in their sports.

Unfortunately, my reference to Tom Moore did not land the way I expected. She was offended. What she heard was that I was suggesting she could never reach Tom Moore's level of horsemanship, as though I were placing a ceiling on her potential. That was never my intention. I was not telling her to stop striving to improve, and I certainly was not saying she was not a good rider. She *is* a good rider.

What I was trying to communicate was something much more nuanced. No matter how much I practice basketball, I will never have the skill set of Michael Jordan. He is a true outlier, a rare combination of physical ability, instinct, and mental toughness that simply does not come around often. A freak of nature, for lack of a better phrase. That reality does not make effort pointless, and it does not make improvement irrelevant. It simply means that we all have different ceilings in different areas, and that is normal.

To me, that realization has always been grounding and even comforting. It creates space for ambition without self-punishment. It allows you to work hard without constantly feeling behind. To her, in that moment, it felt discouraging.

That disconnect made me stop and think more carefully about how riders hear messages about potential, limits, and success. It also made me realize how often reality-based statements are interpreted as permission to quit, when they are actually meant to remove unnecessary pressure.

We all have strengths. We all have areas that come more naturally. We should absolutely strive to be the very best equestrian we can be. But we should not expect to be a superstar at every single aspect of the sport, nor should we allow frustration to take hold when something does not come easily, even with effort.

That lesson is why this chapter exists. Not to discourage ambition, but to organize it. Not to lower standards, but to make them personal, realistic, and sustainable. When riders understand this distinction, they stop fighting themselves and start progressing with clarity.

COMMON MENTAL TRAPS THAT DERAIL PROGRESS

Once comparison takes hold, several predictable mental traps begin to appear. Riders start confusing visibility with success, assuming that the names they see most often or the barns that post the most are automatically further ahead or more accomplished. Others measure themselves against inherited advantages such as family operations, financial backing, or long-established reputations, without accounting for the difference in starting lines. Many also fall into the belief that ambition requires identical outcomes, that wanting to be great means wanting the same career path, titles, or timeline as someone else.

These assumptions are rarely conscious, but they are powerful. They pull riders out of their own process and place their focus on standards that were never theirs to meet.

DEFINING YOUR PERSONAL WIN

One of the most effective ways to counter these mental traps is to define success intentionally before entering the ring. A personal win does not need to be obvious or ribbon-based to be meaningful. On a given day, a good ride might mean riding with confidence instead of hesitation, executing transitions more accurately, presenting a greener horse quietly and correctly, or staying mentally present rather than riding defensively.

When riders clarify what matters to them in advance, their rides become more deliberate. Decisions are cleaner. Body language is more confident. Horses respond to that clarity immediately. Progress becomes measurable in ways that actually support long-term growth.

WHAT THE JUDGE ACTUALLY EVALUATES

The judge does not know your backstory. They do not know what you are rebuilding, refining, or proving this season. They evaluate what is presented in that moment, on that day. They reward what shows up. They do not reward effort that did not translate into performance.

This is not a criticism. It is the reality of judged competition. Riders who understand this stop riding with apology and start riding with alignment. Confidence comes from presenting what you have honestly and intentionally, rather than attempting to perform someone else's narrative.

DIFFERENT PATHS, DIFFERENT DESTINATIONS

Different paths can lead to the same ring, but they do not have to lead to the same destination. Know who you are. Know what you are working with. Know why you are there. Then work relentlessly inside that truth.

You do not need to copy someone else's career or goals. You need to build what fits you. When you do that well, success tends to show up in the ways that actually matter.

10

OUTRIDING FEAR AND WHY OWNING IT IS THE FASTEST WAY FORWARD

Let's cut through the noise. Fear is the single biggest thing holding riders back. Not the horse, not the trainer, not the judge. I'm not going to sugarcoat this. I'm not talking about the abstract stuff like fear of failure, embarrassment, or letting someone down. I mean real, physical fear. The fear that hits when you are actually on the horse. Most riders will never admit it, but I guarantee it is affecting your riding, your learning, and your horse. Fear is debilitating, both figuratively and physically. The worst mistake is denying it or pretending you are above it. You are not. Neither am I. If you can admit it, you can change it.

FEAR: WHY IT'S NORMAL, WHY IT'S NECESSARY

A healthy amount of fear is normal, if you are not at least a little bit scared, you are probably not taking this seriously enough. When you climb on a one-thousand-pound animal with a mind of its own and ask it to perform a complicated set of tasks, respect is not optional. It is mandatory for survival.

Denial, however, is just asking for trouble. Fear is not a weakness or a sign that you do not belong here. It means you care, it means you understand what is at stake, and it means you are paying attention. The best riders out there are not made by the absence of fear. They are made by how they use it. Real riders treat fear as feedback. They take it in as information, not a stop sign. If you let it teach you, you will keep moving forward.

WHEN FEAR GOES ROGUE AND HOW IT SHOWS UP

Fear that is not acknowledged will worm its way into everything you do. It shows up as tension, hesitation, avoidance, or a thousand little excuses. Sometimes it even shows up as regression, when riders go backward in their skills or confidence and can't quite figure out why. If you find yourself "just being cautious," overthinking every cue, fixating on everything could go wrong or holding your breath until you leave the ring, you are not actually riding. You are just surviving. And here is the harsh truth: your horse feels it the most. Horses read tension like it is printed on your forehead. When you are nervous, they get the message loud and clear. You are telegraphing your anxiety straight through the saddle and reins, and your horse has no choice but to react.

HOW FEAR LIMITS LEARNING

This is where it really becomes a problem. Fear blocks the very things that would make you less afraid, learning, building new skills, taking instruction, and improving as a rider. You cannot absorb information or try something new if you are busy trying to control your nerves or keep yourself safe. If you are not honest about being scared, your instructor cannot help you. Your horse ends up paying the price for your silence. Here is the tough love. If you can't admit your fear, you are either lying to yourself or you need to find a new hobby. That is the reality. You cannot train what you refuse to face.

ADMIT IT AND EVERYTHING GETS EASIER

Everything changes the moment a student admits, "I am scared." Now there is something to work with. Progress can happen. I have been there myself. I have the injuries and scars to prove it. The hardest part was not physical recovery. It was finally admitting to myself that I was not invincible. The best riders are not the ones who never get scared. They are the ones who are honest, coachable, and willing to do something about it. That is why they keep improving year after year, while others stall out.

THE SCIENCE OF SETBACK

Fear after an injury or a traumatic experience is not a character flaw. It is biology. Your brain and body are wired to protect you. Fight or flight kicks in. Muscle memory can get hijacked by a bad experience, and trauma can literally reshape your responses if you let it fester. If you do not address that fear, it becomes the filter through which you see every ride. Suddenly you are not just riding your horse, you are riding your anxiety and second-guessing every move.

BREAKING THE CYCLE: ACTION, NOT AVOIDANCE

You do not wait for fear to magically pass. You get back on, you ride, and you face it one step at a time. Start by picking the right horse and the right situation for your comeback. Make sure you have the right support. Do not try to be a hero and go it alone. Use your trainer or a mental coach who actually gets it. Visualize success before you get in the saddle. Make this a daily ritual, not just something you do when you are desperate. Celebrate every small win. Do not obsess over some big, dramatic comeback. Build your confidence one ride at a time. If you are really stuck, get help. This is not about "just think positive." Sometimes you need a sports psychologist, a therapist, or another professional who can dig you out of the hole.

MY STORY: INJURY, HUMILITY, RECOVERY

I have had plenty of injuries in my lifetime, most of them horse related and most of them somehow my fault. However, when I was thirty, I had what I would call a freak accident. I was riding a very kind, small child's horse who did absolutely nothing wrong in this story. We were cantering, and I asked him to walk. His hind foot slipped forward and got caught in his front shoe, causing him to abruptly fall head first to the ground. I stayed in the saddle, but once we were on the ground, I made a terrible decision. I decided to get off while he was still struggling to get back up. I put my hand on the ground to push myself up and off of him, and at the same time he got up and rolled me over my own outstretched arm.

The result was a compound fracture of my wrist that required surgery. I now have nine screws and a plate in my right wrist. I have permanently lost full mobility and rotation in that wrist, along with roughly fifty percent of my grip strength. I mentioned my age earlier because up until that point, I was a fearless trainer in my twenties who genuinely believed I was invincible. This injury shattered that illusion.

The recovery was long and painful. I could not move the fingers for over a month. I could not even put my hair in a ponytail by myself. It was three months before I could hold even the lightest object, which meant holding reins was completely out of the question. It was six months before I could work a horse using two hands. I went to physical therapy three days a week for a full year just to be able to flex my wrist forward and back. My doctor told me that with the severity of the injury and the permanent damage, it would take two years before I even felt normal again, and that it would never be the same normal I knew before.

I want to be clear about something. Permanent damage to my wrist and hand is actually pretty lucky when you consider what could have happened. It could have been my head, my pelvis, or my leg. However, the level of seriousness of the injury is not the point of this story. The point is that it forced me to confront the reality that I could get seriously hurt and that I was not invincible. Some of that realization is healthy. It keeps you from doing reckless and unnecessary things. But for someone who had never allowed fear to limit her riding career, this was a big deal.

When I went back to working horses the way I had before, I absolutely thought about the potential risks every time I put my foot in the stirrup. For a while, those thoughts limited me. I was no longer fully focused on the horse in front of me and how I could help them. Instead, I was focused on what could potentially go wrong and all the ways I could get hurt. I mentioned this to my dad, who is not exactly known for his emotional sensitivity. He matter of factly said to me, "Listen, if you can't get past being scared of falling off a horse or getting hurt while you're supposed to be training them, you need to find a different career."

That was not going to happen. So over the next few months, I did some serious soul searching. I let the horses help me recover by trusting them again and by remembering why I love doing this for a living. It worked. I did get past it. That being said, I am no longer interested in riding the wildest or toughest horses the way I did when I was younger, and I do not see that as a bad thing. That is maturity. That is experience. I have nothing to prove by being fearless. I learned how to respect a little fear, how to move past major fear, and how to move on without letting it define me.

REBUILDING CONFIDENCE AND IDENTITY

You are not defined by the accident, by being scared, or by the worst thing that has ever happened to you in the ring. You are defined by what you do next. The way you talk about it matters. Say it out loud: "That happened. It's over. I am still a competitor." The past only has the power you give it.

Every single top rider you admire has been taken down physically, mentally, or both. The difference is that they get back up. They do not pretend they are bulletproof. They do not let fear be the anchor that drags them down. Instead, they use it as fuel. They ask for help, they admit when they are struggling, and they do not let pride keep them stuck.

THE CHALLENGE: OWN IT, DON'T LET IT OWN YOU

You get one shot at this sport. You get one reputation. Do not let a single fall, or even ten, keep you on the sidelines for good. The comeback is what people remember. It is what you will remember most about yourself. If you love your horse, you owe it to them to become a better, braver rider. Lead from the front, do not shrink from fear. Your horse will thank you, your progress will speak for itself, and your love for the sport will come back stronger than ever.

11

HOW CHAMPIONS ENTER AND HOW TO BREAK THROUGH WHAT'S HOLDING YOU BACK

"Every time you enter the show ring, the judge is rooting for you. Really."

I say it often because it is the truth. A judge's job is to find a winner, and you can help the judge by showing up with intention, presence, and awareness. Many riders underestimate how much influence they have before they ever complete their first pass. Your entrance is the moment when the judge begins forming an impression of you, your horse, and your readiness to compete. Judges genuinely want to see you shine, and we want to reward great rides, but riders often sabotage their own impact in the first few seconds simply because they do not understand how much weight the entrance carries.

Technically we are not supposed to judge until the gate closes and judges adhere to the rule, but the reality is that our eyes are already evaluating. Your class begins the moment you step through the gate. Everything about your entrance shapes how the judge perceives you. Perception may not be everything, but it matters more than you probably think. Your posture, energy, timing, and connection with your horse all speak before you ever ask for your first transition. And yes, judges are absolutely watching. We are not counting mistakes yet, but we are gathering impressions and noting who appears competitive, composed, and confident.

The first impression zone is incredibly powerful. By the time you and your horse reach your first turn, most judges already have early favorites in mind. We notice riders who hesitate, riders who appear disconnected from their horse, riders who look unsure, and riders who appear overly tense. We also notice the opposite. Riders who enter with clarity and poise catch our attention instantly. Riders who look prepared, connected, and intentional stand out. A strong entrance does not require flash and drama. It requires presence. When you step into the ring like you belong there, you automatically place yourself in the judge's "watch closely" category. It may only take a few seconds, but those seconds can set the tone for your entire class.

Everyone wants to look confident and composed when they enter the ring, but they often have no idea what their body language is communicating. Nerves take over, awareness drops, and the ride begins with energy they never intended. I have seen talented riders shrink at the exact moment they should expand, and I have seen less naturally gifted riders command attention simply because they understood how to present themselves the moment they came in. Presence is not a personality trait. It is a skill. Once you understand how to cultivate it, you will begin entering the ring like a rider who expects to be taken seriously.

Judges form an impression from the instant you cross the threshold into the ring. Your posture, your focus, your timing, and your connection with your horse all communicate something long before you make your first full pass. The riders who consistently stand out do not simply trot in. They arrive. They have their shoulders back, their eyes forward, and their minds anchored. Their energy is steady and grounded, and their entrance immediately puts the judge at ease. Horses take their cues from this type of rider, and judges do too. It is quiet confidence, not theatrics, that elevates an entrance.

If you feel like your rides are frequently overlooked, your entrance may be part of the problem. Riders often start off with slouched posture, tight shoulders, or timid energy without realizing how much this undermines their presence. Entering too slowly or scanning the ring nervously creates a sense of hesitation. Appearing disconnected from your horse in the first strides sends the message that you are not ready. These patterns usually come from nerves, pressure, or lack of awareness. Once you understand what your entrance communicates, you can redirect that energy into something far more effective.

Champion presence is not fake confidence. It is grounded, purposeful energy. Exhibitors who enter with presence hold balanced posture without stiffness, keep their eyes engaged and purposeful, and bring a calm, forward-moving intention into the ring. They look like they understand why they are there. Their horses pick up on that clarity and respond to it. These riders do not hope the judge sees them. They make it easy for the judge to notice them. A strong entrance is both a visual statement and a psychological trigger. You do not need to feel one hundred percent confident to enter like a champion, but entering like a champion often allows the confidence to arrive more quickly.

Your entrance matters because it sets the tone for everything that follows. When you come in with clarity and presence, the judge understands immediately that you are in control of your performance. You do not have to convince us later. You already opened the class with a strong message. That same message is sent to yourself. A deliberate entrance signals to your own mind and body that you are ready. It signals to your horse that you are steady and prepared. A weak entrance often results in a shaky start, but a strong entrance gives you momentum.

Even a brilliant ride can begin on the wrong foot if the entrance is chaotic, rushed or inconsiderate. Riders frequently rush to the gate, crowd the entrance, or cluster too closely because they believe being first in gives them an advantage. It does not. Let me repeat that, it does not give them an advantage. Judges watch you enter no matter where you fall in the order. Crowding the gate is one of the biggest pet peeves among judges. It looks frantic, it disrupts flow, and it creates safety issues. It is not competitive and in fact, it is unaware and worse, a safety hazard. A true winner enters with space, respect, and composure. Another major mistake is making your pass too close to the judge. Cutting within arm's reach is never impressive. It undermines your presentation because it prevents us from seeing your horse clearly and forces us to focus on safety instead of evaluating your ride. Confident riders present themselves from a distance that allows us to evaluate their horse with ease.

You can begin building entrance presence long before show day. One of the simplest tools is a trigger phrase that grounds your energy. Choose a short statement that captures how you want to feel when you enter the ring and repeat it consistently. "Let's go." "I'm ready for this." "Presence and poise." The consistency creates a neurological cue that shifts your energy automatically toward clarity and control. Another valuable tool is video feedback. Film yourself riding as if you are entering the ring and watch it back with a critical eye. Ask yourself whether you look confident, steady, and focused. If not, make adjustments and try again. You can visualize entering major venues like Freedom Hall or Oklahoma City while doing this exercise. It trains your nervous system to associate an entrance with readiness and composure.

You can take this further by reviewing footage of your

actual classes. Study your entrances the way a judge would. Notice the energy you bring in the first few strides. If you are unsure how you appear, ask your trainer or a judge you trust for honest feedback. Then apply what you learn the next time you practice your entrance on your horse. This creates a feedback loop that strengthens your presentation each time you show.

WHEN YOU BLOW THE ENTRANCE (AND WHY IT'S NOT THE END)

Now let's address the moment no one wants to talk about, even though it happens to every rider eventually, even the best, you blow the entrance. The timing is off, you canter instead of trotting in, your horse hesitates, you misjudge spacing, or something simply doesn't go according to the plan you've rehearsed a hundred times.

The judge is not supposed to count the mistake, so do not let that moment send you into a spiral. Technically, we cannot score anything until the gate closes, and judges take that rule seriously. Your entrance creates an impression, yes, but the error itself is not the determining factor. So do not freak out. Do not assume you're out of the running. And absolutely do not throw away a class that is still very much winnable.

A blown entrance only becomes a disaster when the rider mentally collapses. The judge may forget it in seconds, but the rider who panics will carry it through every pass. Don't let that be you. The riders who stay competitive after a messy entrance all share one skill: rapid recovery. They reset immediately, reconnect with their horse, and shift their focus back to riding the class in front of them, not the entrance behind them.

HERE IS HOW A PROFESSIONAL RESETS:

1. **Breathe and reorganize.**

   - Don't stiffen, don't rush, don't apologize with your body language. Fix your line, settle your horse, and get into the flow efficiently and quietly.

2. **Refuse to assign meaning.**

   - A poor entrance doesn't mean you are out. It doesn't mean the judge marked you down. It doesn't mean other riders now look better. Let the moment pass and move on.

3. **Ride the rest of the class like you're the one to beat.**

   - If anything, a blown entrance should make you sharper. Clean passes, forward energy, poise in traffic, strong positioning, clear communication. Show the judge why you belong at the top.

4. **Stay emotionally disciplined.**

   - Your ability to recover from small mistakes is part of what separates competitive riders from recreational ones. Anyone can look confident when everything goes right. Champions look confident when it doesn't go right.

5. **Remember the rule of winners:**

   - Ride like the class is always winnable. Because it is. You'd be shocked how many classes are won by the riders who simply didn't quit on themselves when something went sideways.

TELL YOUR STORY YOUR WAY

A mistake is not the story of your ride. It is a moment in your ride. And the judge is more concerned with your total performance than the split second where things weren't perfect. Recovery is a competitive skill. Train it, own it, and use it.

A strong entrance is not luck. It is preparation. And once you master it, you begin every class with an advantage. You do not need to be perfect to ride like a champion. You only need to enter with purpose, poise, and the belief that you belong in the ring. And you do.

DR. AMANDA O'KEEFE MURCHISON

Amanda on CH Spread The Word, winning the Adult Three Gaited Show Pleasure World Champion of Champions.

Dr. Amanda O'Keefe Murchison is a textbook example of a rider who has strategically mastered the art of the attention-grabbing entrance. In this section, she shares insight into her show ring preparation and the systems she uses to compete at the highest level.

Amanda has been caring for and riding horses since before she could walk. American Saddlebreds have been a part of her life since she was eight. She has competed successfully at every level of the sport. Her show ring success speaks for itself. For reference, the Adult Three-Gaited Show Pleasure division is consistently the largest division at the World Championship Horse Show, making success at the top level especially difficult to achieve. In this division, Amanda has earned an impressive seven World Champion titles in qualifying classes on five different horses. She has also won the Adult Three-Gaited Show Pleasure World Champion of Champions title twice aboard WCC CH Spread The Word. Additionally, she has earned three Reserve World Champion of Champions titles, once on CH Spread The Word, once on One Rare Moment and once on Monnington's Prima Ballerina.

She is known not only for her results, but for her sharp ring strategy, unmistakable presence and of course, for her signature white day coat. Amanda captures a judge's attention regardless of which horse she is riding that day. I asked her to share her approach to preparation, her routines before and during competition, and how she sets and manages goals. I am grateful to her for so clearly and generously explaining the systems behind her success.

MENTAL PREPARATION

By Dr. Amanda O'Keefe Murchison

To me, mental preparation has to happen long before you ever go into the ring. It is something you work on consistently so that when it is time to show, you are ready. Trying to fully prepare mentally once you arrive at the horse show or right before your class is not going to work.

The most important part of mental preparedness for me is clearly distinguishing between what I can control and what I cannot. The more I focus on what is within my control, the more mentally prepared I feel.

At the barn, I fully dial in to what my lesson horses, my trainers, and my show horse have to teach me. I stay in a constant state of learning. Everyone has something to teach you if you are open to it. After each ride, I briefly talk through my "aha" moments with my trainers, then I write notes in my phone so I remember them for my next ride, whether that ride is at home or in the show ring.

I also mentally prepare by watching riders I admire. I study their ring strategy, their body position, and their seat. I take in as much as I can.

I set goals for each ride as well. Goals are something I can control. If I do not meet a goal, that is okay, because a goal is not a requirement. I intentionally limit myself to two or three goals that are completely within my control, such as remembering to sit back in transitions.

I also work out. My horse works every day, and I believe I should too. Knowing I have physically prepared helps me feel mentally prepared.

When I get to the show, especially at highly competitive shows, I do the following:

1. I get ready in the hotel and listen to fast music that makes me feel confident and energized.
2. I remind myself again of what I can control. I talk my goals through with my trainers before my class, never more than three. I visualize my class,

including my must-dos, my goals, and my strategic ring placement and transitions.

3. While waiting to warm up, I practice mindfulness and anti-anxiety exercises, such as naming five things I see, four things I physically feel, three things I hear, and so on.
4. I always stretch before a class. My trainer, Kristen Cater has exercise bands at the shows and I use them to warm up my muscles every time.
5. When I get on to warm up, I take a deep breath and focus only on my horse and my team. I never watch anyone else warm up. It is not about them. It is about my horse, my team, and me.
6. I remind myself of my preparation and intentionally work to feel confident. One of my professors during my doctoral program, Dr. Russ Quaglia, said, "Fear is enthusiasm in need of an attitude adjustment." I use that as a mantra.
7. Most importantly, on the biggest stages, I remind myself how fortunate I am to be there. My dad always said, "Inside looking out." He meant *you get to be* on the inside of the ring looking out, not on the outside looking in. Being on the inside looking out is a gift and a blessing, and not everyone gets to do it. That phrase reminds me how grateful I am to compete in this sport, with these horses and these people. That gratitude grounds me and gives me perspective when it matters most.

12

THE WALK. PLANNING, POSITIONING, AND NOT LOSING THE CLASS

After you have nailed your entrance and executed your passes during the first trot, it is walk time. Sometimes it is the dreaded gait, sometimes it is a welcome breather, but in either case, ring strategy becomes essential. The planning, timing, and placement of your walk can absolutely affect the outcome of your class, and it should never be underestimated.

Believe me, many classes are lost at the walk. Not because the horse was not good enough, but because the rider did not plan properly or lacked awareness of what their horse needed at that moment.

The walk is not just the walk. Yes, it is a judged gait, but just as important is the fact that how you execute the walk directly impacts the quality of your next transition. Being familiar with how your horse feels about walking, and where in the ring they walk best, is invaluable. Equally important is tuning into their energy and mindset during the class, regardless of what division you are showing in.

Most trainers teach riders to finish their pass when the walk is called from the trot. It is a smart strategy as the judge gets to see your full pass, and most horses tend to settle better walking on the ends of the arena. That one move solves two problems. Even better, it often means your next transition, usually to the canter, will happen in the turn or just as you come out of it, which is where most horses are most comfortable departing.

Since the judge is typically watching the rail directly in front of them, not the turn, you have a chance to get your canter lead quietly and cleanly before you are back in full view. You are solid. You are comfortable. You look like you have it together. This is ring strategy in action.

Now, I am not saying everyone is going to mess up their canter transition. What I am saying is I have watched hundreds, and I mean hundreds, of riders lose a class because they rushed into the canter. They got nervous, the horse responded to that energy, and suddenly what could have been a clean, composed transition has now turned into a scene. So even if you are a confident rider on a seasoned show horse, ask yourself, why risk it?

Unexpected things happen all the time at horse shows. If you can help it, finish your pass, walk the turn, and take your canter from a thoughtful, prepared place. Not to sound like a broken record, but remember judges want to see you succeed. We are watching you at the walk, and we are rooting for you in the transitions, so help us out. Plan ahead. Make ring strategy a priority.

Yes, there is a limit to how many extra passes you can make before walking without annoying the judge. Finishing one pass? Great. Two? Maybe. But three or more under the guise of finding a spot on the rail? We see you. And no, we are not fooled. If you are avoiding the walk for too long, we notice and it will affect how we evaluate your ride.

Now, some of you might be thinking, "But what if it is a big class and the turns are crowded?" Fair. It happens, I have been there. My advice? At the very least, trot past where the judge is watching and then walk. Many times, this will be around the halfway point on the rail. That way, you can walk into the turn and still take your transition in the corner where your horse is most likely to succeed.

If walking down the rail and taking your canter directly in front of the judge is unavoidable, here is what you do: stay calm. Reassure your horse with confident, quiet energy. Do not rush your departure. Maybe say a little prayer. Judges know someone has to take their canter in front of them, it is not the end of the world. As long as you have planned your walk, remained composed, and set yourself up for a clean, collected transition, you are not going to annoy the judge.

KNOW WHEN IT IS TIME TO WALK: AVOID FRUSTRATING EVERYONE IN CENTER RING

Let us talk about those extra passes after the walk is called. When you continue completing full rails after the announcer has clearly called for the walk, it crosses the line from smart ring strategy into frustrating the judge, the ringmaster, the announcer and putting the rest of the class at a disadvantage.

At that point, everyone is waiting on you to transition, and it is important to remember: the walk is a required gait. It must be executed in some form. While we understand the reasons a rider might delay the walk, particularly with horses who do not settle well, it still does not justify making an entire ring full of horses and people wait for an extended period of time.

We just discussed, there are ways to manage horses who do not walk well, but they require planning, awareness, and a willingness to assess where the rest of the class is and how long they have been walking. What you want to avoid is taking so long to transition that the judge is forced to call for the next gait before you ever walk. In most cases, that will result in not having performed the required gait and yes, that can affect your placing.

I was judging on a panel with Jim Cherry, a respected and very experienced judge, when a class came up that every judge has dealt with at some point. One exhibitor took an excessive amount of time to come down to the walk after the call had been made.

As judges do, we discussed it. Jim explained how he handles that situation, and his approach stuck with me because it is measured, reasonable, and fair to the entire class.

Once the walk has been called and he has had adequate time to observe every other entry walking, his attention naturally shifts. Not because the other horses are finished being judged, and not because their walk is cut short. They have done exactly what was asked of them.

From that point forward, he simply turns his focus to the exhibitor who has not yet transitioned down to the walk.

It would not be fair to compress the evaluation of compliant horses or move the class forward prematurely because one rider chose to ignore the call and continue circling. The delay belongs solely to the exhibitor who did not come down when asked.

This approach keeps the judging honest. It respects the horses and riders who followed instructions. And it addresses the issue without drama or confrontation.

If you are still trotting when the walk has been called, understand this: you are no longer blending into the class. You are now the rider under the judge's primary attention. Every step, every moment, every decision is being observed while everyone else waits. This is not a penalty. It is a consequence.

Effective ring strategy is not about squeezing in one more pass or testing how far you can push a call. It is about awareness, professionalism, and respect for the class as a whole. Judges notice that.

Be strategic. Be self aware. And know when it is time to walk.

And finally, a quick reminder: the walk is a judged gait. You must perform it in some form in every division except Roadster and a couple Hackney divisions. If you stop and stand through the entire walk, you have skipped a required gait and yes, your placing can absolutely be affected.

It is frustrating as a judge to want to tie the best horse first and not be able to because the rider did not plan ahead for the walk or the transition. Do not be that person.

Another thing while we are on the topic of canter transitions: please wait for the rider in front of you to take their canter, within reason, of course. The judge does not want to see you run up on the back of another horse mid transition. If you are in a crowd, it is completely acceptable and actually preferred that you wait a moment before making your move. Give the horse in front of you time to depart, establish its gait, and move forward.

Why? For one, it prevents collisions. But just as importantly, it saves you from having to make an awkward, abrupt turn to avoid them which often throws off your horse's balance and leads to mistakes like switching leads or scrambling into the gait. No one looks composed darting around another horse mid transition. What looks calm and confident from the center of the ring is a rider who knows how to time their move. Even a few seconds of patience can completely change the quality of your canter and your presentation.

Again, it is imperative that you understand your horse's behavior and preferences, or at the very least, listen to what your trainer says your horse needs. For example, if your horse gets impatient once the announcer calls for the canter, you should plan to be the leader of the pack and take your transition first. If your horse tends to canter faster than most, you will want to get ahead of the crowd so you do not have to awkwardly pass other horses right away and make your speed the most noticeable thing about your ride.

Conversely, if your horse canters on the slower side or does not appreciate other horses flying by, you are better off waiting until the bulk of the crowd has gone so you can make a clean, calm transition in open space.

Just a little bit of wherewithal, planning ahead, and proper execution can give you the edge when the judge is signing their card. These are the kinds of choices that make us think of you fondly when we are deciding where to write in your number, instead of being annoyed by your choices.

Now, what if the horse in front of you during the canter transition is acting up or struggling to get its lead? There comes a point when you simply cannot wait any longer, you have to canter. The first thing you need to know is this: the judge understands. We know what is happening. We know it is not your fault or your horse's fault, but how you handle the situation is on you.

So what do you do? Stay calm. This is not a dealbreaker for your placing. If you know your horse can reliably take its lead off the rail, you can quietly move toward the center of the ring and canter off. Or, if it suits your horse better, take your lead on the rail and guide your horse smoothly, not abruptly, around the one that is having trouble. You can even walk up just past them, get back to the rail in front of them, and take your canter from there. Whatever you choose, the most important thing is to stay composed and make the decision that best suits your horse.

Now let us flip the scenario. If you are the one ahead, and someone behind you does not wait, runs up too close, or causes your horse to make a mistake, again, the judge understands. A judge who is a true horseman knows that a horse being put in a difficult or unsafe situation can lead to a mistake that was nearly unavoidable and most of us will forgive that.

But how you recover from that drive by matters. If your horse cannot mentally regroup, or if you get so rattled that your horse feeds off your energy and starts compounding the mistake, that is when it starts to cost you. You cannot always control the traffic, but you can control how you respond to it. And that comes down to knowing your horse, training for composure, and riding like the confident, prepared competitor you came to be.

At the end of the day, showing like you planned it is not about controlling every variable in the ring. You cannot control the traffic, the mistakes other riders make, or exactly how the class plays out. What you can control is how prepared you are, how quickly you think, and how steady you stay when things get busy. Judges remember the riders who make smart decisions in real time, protect their horse, and try their best to not let the picture completely fall apart, even when the class gets chaotic.

In the next chapter, we are going to take all of this one step further and look at what happens when the announcer calls for the reverse and you do it like you planned it.

13

THE REVERSE, THE REVEAL

The reverse can be one of the most telling moments in any class. By the time the announcer calls for it, the first act is over. The judge likely has a good idea how they want to place the class if nothing were to change the second direction, at the least they have got a working list of standouts, and a sense of who is showing up with presence and who is blending into the crowd. Do not make the mistake of thinking the reverse is just a routine transition and nothing can change. The second direction is where the judge looks to confirm decisions, decides to reshuffle the order, or reconsider the card entirely. It is also where riders lose ground without even realizing it.

Every rider knows the reverse is coming, yet many fail to treat it like the opportunity it truly is. It is a deceptively simple maneuver that exposes your focus, your poise, your ring awareness, and whether you and your horse are still mentally in the game. Some competitors let their precision slip and their energy diminish, while the ones who stay sharp rise above the pack. The reverse is not about flair. It is about clarity. The judge is not watching where you reverse as much as how you reverse.

A confident, well-timed move communicates intention and control. A sloppy or hesitant one communicates the opposite.

THE REVERSE THAT SEALED THE DEAL

Matt Shiflet and WGC CH I'm Lookin' At You on their victory pass after winning the Five Gaited World Grand Championship in 2020. Photo by Howard Schatzberg.

A perfect example of how a reverse can tip the scales came in the 2020 Five-Gaited World Grand Championship, when WGC CH *I'm Lookin' At You* won with his past trainer, Matt Shiflet, aboard. Ironically, and lucky for me, this outstanding horse is now in my barn.

Matt is arguably one of the greatest showmen of our time, and very possibly of all time. That night was a masterclass. As I keep stating throughout this book, a tremendous amount can be learned simply by observing people like this with a keen eye and an open mind. I, for one, took a lot away from that class.

As with most five-gaited classes, you will hear a lot about the slow gait and the rack being the deciding factors, and that is a fair observation. However, in this class, one could argue the moment that truly separated *I'm Lookin' At You* from the rest was the way Matt guided him through the middle on the most well-timed, dynamic reverse, followed by a committed trot through the center of the ring. You could even argue that the reverse and trot in the workout were even more impressive.

Matt knew exactly where his horse excelled. He understood that this was the moment to make a statement, not by forcing brilliance, but by letting the horse show strength, balance, and command right where judges are watching most closely.

And while I was not judging that night, I would say it worked. He left the arena with the blanket of roses and the bragging rights. That is not luck. That is strategy.

THE RIGHT HORSE. THE RIGHT CLASS. THE RIGHT NIGHT.

> *"Showing a horse is like driving in rush-hour traffic. You have to look ahead, but just as importantly, you have to know what's happening behind you. Who's coming up, what move they're about to make, and how that affects your next decision."*
> — Matt Shiftlet

In speaking with Matt about ring strategy, he compared showing a horse to driving on the freeway during rush hour. Of course, you have to be looking ahead to make smart decisions and know when it is time to change lanes. But just as important is knowing what is happening behind you. You need to be aware of who is coming up on you, what moves they might make, and how those decisions affect the flow of the class.

Matt pointed out that sometimes the smartest strategy is simply staying in your lane. Not every moment calls for trying to pass your competition. In fact, unnecessary cutting disrupts the class, and makes it harder for everyone to show effectively.

He acknowledged that restraint can be difficult, especially for competitive riders, but discipline in these moments often sets the class up for success.

He also emphasized that cutting too much, or cutting too soon, can work directly against you by putting yourself too close to the judge. At that point, the judge cannot properly see your horse and often cannot see the rest of the field either. And if the judge cannot see you, they cannot tie you.

Along those same lines, Matt talked about the importance of patience, timing and reading your horse. Sometimes delaying your next move is the smartest choice you can make. You have to give your horse a moment to settle and catch some fire before asking for more. Rushing a pass rarely creates brilliance. Waiting for the right moment often does.

Matt was also very clear about one fundamental truth: when you are showing, you are riding for the judge. They are the ones deciding your fate. Every decision you make in the ring should put your horse in a better position to be evaluated in the best possible light. Strategy, placement, and timing all exist to serve that purpose.

That said, he acknowledged that there is a small percentage of nights when something special happens. On the right horse, in the right class, on the right night, the crowd begins to feel the horse's presence and charisma. When that energy builds and the audience gets behind you, that is when you can ride for the crowd and truly put on a show. On those rare nights, the roar of the crowd and the judge's decision often align, and you hear your number called out first.

When discussing the reverse specifically on *I'm Lookin' At You*, Matt explained that he knew the reverse was one of that horse's greatest strengths. Even in deep competition, he believed the horse could capture attention by executing a bold, dynamic reverse through the middle. While the reverse is sometimes underestimated, Matt emphasized that there is an art to it. You should already have a plan before you finish cantering the first direction of the ring.

Once you come down from the canter, you need to be sitting on go, but that does not mean rushing the reverse. You have to wait until your horse is ready to deliver it with the level of energy you planned for and to be sure you are not trotting straight into a traffic jam. Timing and placement are everything. Done correctly, that moment can be the spark that carries you and your horse all the way to the winner's circle.

I often walk away from conversations with Matt feeling inspired to be a better horse trainer, showman and teacher, and this one was no different. He approaches the show ring with an unmistakable optimism and a natural charisma that supports his belief in what success should look like. More importantly, he has a clear vision of how a class should unfold and consistently finds a way to execute that vision when it matters. He is a big-picture thinker, and there is no question that those traits have played a role in his success.

Matt has clearly spent time analyzing what separates good performances from winning ones and how to make those moments repeatable under pressure. That level of intentionality is something I admire in any competitor. After all, isn't that what most of us are striving for? The ability to think clearly, show decisively, and deliver our best performance when it counts.

TIMING YOUR REVERSE

A dynamic and attention grabbing reverse. Photo by Howard Schatzberg.

Timing matters as well. Reverse too early before the judge even nods to the ringmaster and you are not being strategic. You are being disruptive. Wait too long and you create a jam that frustrates everyone around you. Neither approach earns respect. The reverse should be calm, organized, and deliberate. It should look like part of your plan, not like you were scrambling for an exit ramp.

Then there is the chaos through the center of the ring. If you cut through without scanning for traffic or without giving yourself enough space, you are not making a bold move. You are volunteering to create a problem directly in front of the judge. We see everything from the center of the ring, including every rushed decision and every near miss. The riders who execute the reverse with composure demonstrate that they are still thinking, still showing, and still competing. It sends a message that you are riding with intention rather than passively surviving the class.

The reverse tells the judge who is still presenting a complete performance and who has mentally checked out. When you reverse with purpose, the message is clear: you came to compete, not coast.

THE LINEUP PASS: YOUR LAST CHANCE TO MAKE IT COUNT

When the announcer calls for the lineup, many riders quietly shut down. They assume the work is done. In reality, this final pass is one of the most overlooked opportunities to influence your placing. While you are making your final trip toward the lineup, the judge is often multitasking. There may be notes to review, rankings to finalize, and decisions still in motion. If the judge is looking down at the card, this is not the time for a dramatic final pass. They are not watching. Get to the lineup smoothly and save the theatrics for when they actually matter.

If the judge is looking up and around the arena, that is your cue. This is your last moment in motion, your final chance to make a clean impression, and your opportunity to remind the judge why you belong at the top. To take advantage of it, you need to know your horse. If your horse rushes into the lineup, do not fight them and do not fuel that energy. Take a breath and let the moment settle. Then make a well timed, dynamic final pass. Dramatic does not win here. Deliberate wins here.

Every horse has quirks, and the lineup exposes them. Some horses cannot line up early without mentally unraveling. Some become restless if they are left on the end too long. Others simply do not handle tight spacing. Know your horse and make decisions that set both of you up for success. If your horse stands better in the middle, time your lineup accordingly. If they need space, take the end. If you know your horse is better backing early, watch a few classes ahead of yours so you know which direction the ringmaster usually starts from. These small decisions help you appear polished, organized, and thoughtful.

In five-gaited classes, another layer of strategy comes into play. If your horse looks best at a slow gait or rack and the moment aligns, you can use that gait in your final pass. Never try to force a moment your horse cannot support. If they have a different idea and want to trot instead of rack, accept it and make it look intentional. Arguing with your horse in the final pass never works in your favor and can bring about a mistake that was completely avoidable. A confident rider adapts instantly and keeps the presentation polished.

There is also the strategy of the slightly delayed lineup pass (not too much delay. As stated, you don't want to make the judge and everyone else wait too long). If the rest of the class charges into line like they are collecting free concert tickets, take a breath and wait. When done correctly, entering a few seconds later gives you open space, clean visibility, and a moment that is all your own. Just be smart. Do not wait so long that you look lost or unprepared. The goal is strategic timing, not distraction.

Strategic timing is powerful and real mastery is knowing when you can own the moment. If you have ever shown against Steve Wheeler, you know exactly what I mean. You cannot out-wait him on the line up pass.

Steve does not just calculate the timing of that pass. He has calculated the timing and precise execution of the entire class for every class. From the first entrance to the lineup, everything is intentional. That awareness shows up in his showmanship, his training, and, ultimately, his results.

The delayed lineup pass is not a last-minute decision for him. It is the natural conclusion of a plan that has been unfolding since the gate opened.

I use the delayed lineup pass myself when the situation calls for it. But when I am in the ring with Steve, I know better. I end up settling for the second-to-last pass. And honestly, if you know me at all I don't concede to much or to too many people, so that choice says a lot about the respect he commands in the show ring.

THE ACTUAL LINEUP: WHERE YOU CAN STILL LOSE

By the time you head into line, most judges already have the class loosely sorted in their minds. The lineup is not usually where winners are created, but it is absolutely where winners can be lost. Horses that cannot stand, riders who panic, and teams that unravel in the final minute often lose ground they had earned earlier. There is nothing more frustrating than having to change your placings or beat your favorite because someone blows the lineup or the back.

A horse that dances, fidgets, or pins its ears may not ruin a class, but a rider who looks overwhelmed or frustrated will. A crooked or rushed backup tells the judge you were not prepared. A stiff jaw, restless feet, or broken connection between horse and rider signals that the polish fell apart before the job was done. On the other hand, a horse that stands quietly, a rider who looks composed, and a team that appears content and capable often seals the deal. Judges notice who finishes the job with professionalism.

Finish like you are still being evaluated, because you are. The class is not over until the judge hands in the card. That last impression might matter more than you think.

WHEN COMPETITION TURNS INTO CHAOS

Healthy ring rivalry can elevate a class. A well-timed pass, a confident expression, or a moment of intensity can add energy and presence. But when competition turns into gamesmanship, it almost always backfires.

Cutting across the ring to block someone, riding another exhibitor like you are attached at the hip, or slipping in so close you could steal a stirrup is not strategy. It is interference. And it becomes a lasting memory for everyone involved, including the judge.

I learned that lesson firsthand in a young horse class at Freedom Hall. I was racking down the rail with my stirrup literally clinking against another trainer's as he passed, having pinned me up against the wall. I am not suggesting it was intentional, but intent does not matter. What matters is how it reads from the middle. And moments like that do not read as competitive or impressive. They read as avoidable and unnecessary. And these types of avoidable, unnecessary moments never help your card.

From the judge's view, these moves rarely look clever. They look frantic. They rattle horses, they annoy the judge, and they create more problems for the rider who initiated them than the rider they were trying to affect. The goal is not to disrupt the class. The goal is to dominate your moment. The best riders shine without creating disorder. They create space when they need it, execute their passes with authority, and let their horse's quality do the talking.

Ride with presence, not panic. Make competitive choices that elevate your ride and keep your horse confident. There is nothing more amateur-looking than throwing away your own ride just to interfere with someone else's. The most impressive riders win with intention and clarity. They create their own lane and stay in it.

ALWAYS PAT YOUR HORSE

More importantly, no matter how the class went, your horse deserves gratitude. They showed up for you, carried you, and gave you what they had that day. They do not understand judges cards or placings. They understand how you make them feel. A simple, genuine pat shows partnership, appreciation, and emotional maturity. Judges notice it. Trainers notice it. Horses feel it. The riders who treat their horses with acknowledgment and respect, win or lose, are the riders we remember for the right reasons.

That pat is not a formality. It is information and it tells your horse, "You did your job." Even when the ride was not perfect. Even when the result stings. Horses that feel appreciated stay willing. Horses that feel blamed shut down, brace, or start protecting themselves. Over time, that difference shows up in consistency, confidence, and longevity.

Gratitude also keeps you honest as a rider. When your first instinct after a class is appreciation instead of frustration, you are less likely to punish the wrong thing, rush to change equipment, or assume the horse failed you. You pause. You reflect. You take responsibility for your part. That mindset creates better horsemen and better results, whether people want to admit it or not.

And yes, judges see more than riders realize. They see how you exit the ring. They see whether disappointment turns into tension on the reins or quiet professionalism. They see riders who acknowledge their horses versus riders who immediately check the card, shake their head, or ride off annoyed. One tells a story of partnership. The other tells a story of entitlement.

Most importantly, your horse earned it. They carried your nerves, your ambition, your mistakes, and your expectations into the ring. A pat costs nothing. But it signals respect, maturity, and leadership. In a sport built on partnership, that matters.

Always pat your horse. Especially on the days you feel disappointed.

STRATEGIC DOWNTIME: THE UNWRITTEN CURRICULUM OF SHOW RING MASTERY

Timeouts and delays can occur at any point in a class, and they are one of the most overlooked elements of show ring performance. In fact, sometimes we, as trainers, even forget to explain to our riders and drivers what our expectations and advice are during a time-out. Then panic sets in when one is called. Let's fix that.

While the judge is not technically evaluating during a time-out, these moments reveal professionalism, poise, and preparation in a way that is impossible to hide. How you handle unexpected downtime can support your performance or quietly sabotage it.

Riders who manage timeouts well immediately locate their trainer and maintain direct communication. Sometimes it is an actual emergency and sometimes it is just a tack adjustment. They do not wander or panic. They stay focused and grounded. They read the room and adjust accordingly. If the environment is tense, they stay calm. If the crowd is loud, they stay centered. Their priority remains their horse, not the noise nor the spectacle.

Your responsibility during a timeout is to protect your horse's mindset and energy. Some horses need to keep walking. Some need distance from the cluster. Others need quiet reassurance. Know what your horse needs and use the timeout to support them rather than agitate them.

Sometimes you will see riders, most often trainers, make passes down the rail or even complete full rounds during a timeout. While some horses genuinely need to move during a timeout, in other cases this is an attempt to get the judge's attention, as if that pass can be counted toward the placing. While a judge can certainly appreciate a nice horse making a quality pass on its own, this tactic should not sway the decision.

In many situations, the crowd gets behind the horse making the pass and responds with enthusiastic cheering. Yes, showmanship and crowd support are part of the sport, but consider this scenario: the timeout is for a cast shoe. The farrier is underneath the horse in the middle of the arena, racing the clock. A horse makes a pass, the crowd erupts, and the horse having its shoe replaced becomes excited and reactive from the noise. At that point, you have jeopardized another exhibitor's five-minute timeout and put the farrier, the handler, and the horse at risk. All for a pass the judge cannot count anyway.

Judges understand that there are times when a horse needs to move or be worked during a timeout, and that is allowed. When it is done in a way that creates disruption or safety concerns, it becomes a problem for everyone.

As the timeout winds down, position yourself thoughtfully. Claim your space on the rail early. Prepare your horse mentally for the restart. Avoid burning unnecessary energy by trotting aimless laps while the judging is paused. Save the best for when the class officially resumes.

These moments do not feel glamorous, but the riders who master them separate themselves from the pack. Managing downtime is part of true show ring mastery. It reflects your awareness, your horsemanship, and your professionalism. The riders who stay composed through every unpredictable moment are the ones who rise to the top.

At every stage of a class, from the first moments on the rail to each transition, the reverse, and the lineup pass, you are revealing who you are as a competitor. None of these moments exist in isolation. Together, they tell the full story of your preparation, your awareness, and your respect for the sport. Riders who succeed at the highest level understand that nothing in the ring is accidental. Every transition, every pause, and every decision either reinforces confidence or exposes cracks. When you ride with intention through the reverse, finish with confidence in the lineup, compete without creating unnecessary disruptions, and manage downtime with professionalism, you separate yourself without saying a word. That is the real advantage. The reveal is not a single moment. It is the sum of how you show up from start to finish, especially when you think no one is watching.

14

HOW TO SHOW LIKE YOU PLANNED IT

Entering the ring with confidence is step one. But the ride does not stop there. Once you are in and the class is underway, how you carry yourself, moment to moment, says just as much about your preparation, awareness, and showmanship as your horse's movement does. And yet, this is where many riders unintentionally give away points, attention, and presence. The truth is, most riders enter the ring with a plan, but the riders who stand out, who stay composed and consistent from start to finish, are the riders who are prepared and confident enough to execute that plan. When you and your horse are truly ready, and you have trained with purpose, you are able to adapt under pressure, stay mentally sharp, and ride with clarity even when things do not go exactly as expected. Confidence in the ring is not about hoping it goes right, it is about being prepared enough to make it go right.

CAN YOU EXECUTE YOUR PLAN UNDER PRESSURE?

We have established that most riders intend to enter the ring with a plan. The real question that separates average riders from exceptional riders is, can you execute that plan under pressure, when it counts, in front of a judge, with everything on the line?

What happens when the energy shifts? When your horse feels a little different than they did in the warm-up ring? When your ring placement is not what you hoped for, or the class dynamics do not allow for the track you visualized? These are the moments where confidence is either confirmed or exposed.

Can you still ride with clarity and presence when your timing is off by even just a stride? Can you stick to your plan or adapt without unraveling when your horse is reacting to the atmosphere? Can you keep showing, cleanly and intentionally, in a way that allows the judge to actually evaluate your performance?

Losing focus, getting reactive, or improvising in a panic immediately disrupts your presentation. If the judge cannot clearly see what your horse is capable of due to tension, distraction, or constant adjusting, we cannot reward you, even if you entered the ring with the best horse in the class.

The reality is that a lot of people can ride well when everything is going right. What gets rewarded in the show ring is not just talent, it is execution. And execution depends on preparation, presence, and the ability to hold yourself together under pressure. Confidence is not about always getting it right, it is about riding in a way that makes your strengths visible, even when things are not perfect.

A REAL EXAMPLE OF EXECUTING UNDER PRESSURE

CH Our Charming Lady & Mary Orr winning the coveted Three Gaited World Grand Championship in 2008 for owners Jack & Donna Finch. Photo by Doug Shiftlet.

One of the strongest examples of executing under pressure comes from world champion trainer and rider Mary Orr, who won the Three Gaited World Grand Championship in her twenties with WGC CH Our Charming Lady. Her approach was built on visualization and strategic planning at a level many equestrians never reach.

In Mary's own words, "WGC CH Our Charming Lady was an incredible horse but she had little to no patience. Her gameness and impatience forced me to visualize and gave me a skill I am not sure I would have developed so quickly at such an early stage of my career. I knew that I had a limited amount of steps and time in between her gaits and therefore I had to have a plan when and where I was going to stop to have a successful class and keep her settled."

Mary created not one plan, but a plan for every possible version of the ride.

"I would go to the ring and plan for every single possible place the announcer would call for the walk in the ring and make a plan. This helped me when I was showing. I knew with one hundred percent certainty what my plan was for each transition. I knew exactly where I wanted to transition and how to get to those spots no matter how the class was called."

Her planning sharpened her focus instead of overwhelming her.

"This plan also helped me with my nerves. I never worried about winning or how to show this horse. I was laser focused on my planning and positioning to set her up for success."

She emphasizes that visualization must be tailored to the horse.

"What I have learned is that each horse visualization needs to be for the particular team. My horse was extremely game and talented so behavioral and positioning was my focus. There could be other horses that need the rider to visualize riding the horse or how to use the leg in the ring. Regardless of what you need to focus on, taking the time to make a plan for me personally cleared my head and helped me really be in the moment with my horse."

Her experience fundamentally changed her as a rider.

"I was always focused and made plans but WGC CH Our Charming Lady changed me as a trainer, rider and performer. I never had gotten to that spot mentally and learned to plan and truly block out everything. Her idiosyncrasies brought me to a different level as a person and rider."

The approach has stuck with her.

"It is a way of life for me now. I do not know how to show without a plan and see the show ring completely differently since that show ring experience. I am not comfortable if I do not make a plan and visualize."

Mary also points out that pressure can sharpen you instead of breaking you.

"Honestly, that mare was challenging that to be safe and successful there was no choice. I find that a little fear can work in your favor. Your body takes over and your brain stays focused. The horse needed me at one hundred percent and visualizing prepared me to be there for her."

Today she teaches visualization to her riders.

"I work constantly with my riders with this in their lessons, on the ground and watching horse shows. I do not know how you can perform at the highest level and not find your personal zone that helps you ride and perform well."

Mary's story is the perfect example of the difference between simply having a plan and actually executing one. Every rider has a vision of the ride they want. True champions create a plan for every version of the ride they might actually get.

COMPETITION WITHOUT CHAOS: RIDE SMART, NOT SCRAPPY

Judges get it. This is a competition. Of course, the right amount of competitive spirit can absolutely produce big results. When that drive goes unchecked, it starts to cost you. It costs your position. It costs your poise. And more often than not, it costs your horse the ability to shine.

One of the most dangerous moments we see in the ring is when riders get too aggressive trying to secure an unblocked pass, the golden moment when their horse is directly in front of the judge without being covered up by another entry. It is a smart goal. We understand why you want to be clearly seen. But when riders try to accomplish this by squeezing between another horse and the judge, riding dangerously close to people, or charging through tight spaces, things can get sketchy fast for the riders, the horses, the judges, and the ringmasters.

It is important to understand, your horse does not look its

best when it is playing chicken with the ringmaster or getting up close and personal with another entry. Crowding another horse does not make you look confident, it makes the whole picture feel tense and chaotic. Horses, like humans, show their best when they are relaxed, forward thinking, and working in the open. When a horse is by itself and not sandwiched between distractions, it is freer to show its motion, its expression, and its personality.

We know this kind of perfect pass is easier said than done, especially in large, fast moving classes. But I promise: if you commit to using your turns as workshops, to truly prepare your horse for what is coming, the ring often opens up like magic. It can feel like the parting of the Red Sea, for lack of a better example. Suddenly, the rail is yours. The pass is blue ribbon worthy. And it looks like you are the only rider in the class.

A huge part of this is learning to make strategic choices in the turn. For example: Do I cut out early to get ahead of the pack? Do I slow up and let the group go so I can come out clean behind them? This is where knowing your horse really matters. What pace do they prefer? Do they stay expressive when there is traffic behind them? Or do they light up when they are out front? These details make a difference. And the best riders have a quiet mastery of them.

COMMANDING THE RING WITHOUT NOISE

You can learn an enormous amount just by watching from the stands. Pay attention to the riders who seem to exist in their own orbit. Even in a crowded ring, they create space. Sometimes they are on the best horse in the class. Sometimes they are not. But either way, they command attention through ring intelligence, composure, and absolute ownership of their plan.

Those are the riders worth studying. I learn something every time I watch them.

When I was a kid, my dad was relentless about one thing: watch Michele McFarlane every chance you get.

She is one of the most accomplished amateurs our industry has ever seen. She did not just break records. She redefined what was possible. Michele was the first woman and only the second amateur to win the Five-Gaited World Grand Championship, and she did not do it once. She won it on three different horses over the course of her career.

Because she was based near San Diego, growing up on the West Coast gave me the rare advantage of watching her often. What stood out was not showiness or excess. It was discipline. Michele rode with deliberate, businesslike precision. Her passes were intentional, direct, and unapologetic. She chose her line and owned it. She did not let traffic move her, pressure rush her, or competition dictate her timing in front of the judge.

There is something powerful about riding as if you are the only one in the ring and executing your plan without interference, distraction, or negotiation. Michele mastered that. And watching her taught me that real ring presence is not loud. It is decisive.

Ring Reset

One-Minute Show Ring Affirmations
Read this before you show to reset your focus, reinforce your standards & remind yourself you can perform under pressure.

1. My turnout is sharp. Clothes fit, boots clean. Presentation is non-negotiable.

2. I enter with intent & presence. I belong and everyone knows it from the first stride.

3. I showcase my horse at the right times & places and let my best moments be seen.

4. I never cut corners, literally or figuratively.

5. If I make a mistake, I reset instantly. No drama, no excuses.

6. My body language says I rise under pressure. I commit, & I expect to be in the winner's circle.

7. I keep my composure every step. No matter what, I finish as strong as I started.

8. I want feedback. I am coachable & adaptable.

9. I represent more than myself. I show up for my barn, my people, for my horse & the standard we set.

10. Every class, every judge, every ride. I treat it like it matters, because it does.

15

EQUITATION. EVERY DETAIL MATTERS

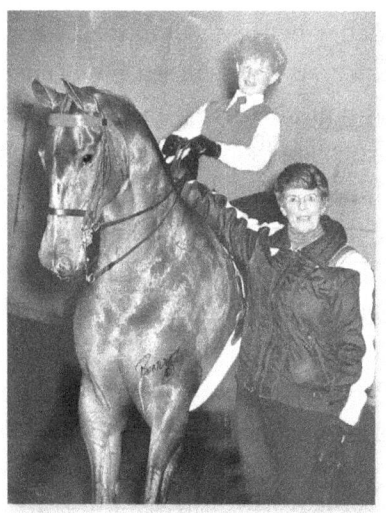

Allison Deardorff on CH Rolls Royce with Mrs. Helen Crabtree, author of Saddle Seat Equitation.

Contrary to popular belief, equitation isn't about how fancy your horse is. It's about how well you ride and how well you present yourself. In this division, the judge isn't scoring your horse's talent. We're judging you.

And the truth is, there are some non-negotiables if you want to be competitive in equitation. No amount of raw riding ability can cover up a sloppy turnout, a stiff frame, or a missed opportunity to show yourself at your best. Equitation demands discipline, attention to detail, and the kind of composure that says, *I'm here to be taken seriously.*

Before we go any further, I want to be very clear about what this chapter is and is not meant to do. This book is not here to teach you how to achieve the most perfect equitation position, measured inch by inch. That is not its purpose. There are already exceptional resources devoted entirely to classical position and mechanics, and I am not trying to replace them.

If your goal is to study Saddle Seat Equitation in its purest, most technical form, there is a definitive text that already exists: *Saddle Seat Equitation* by Helen Crabtree. She was the authority. The guru. The person who shaped how generations of riders understood position, balance, and correctness. That book teaches where your leg belongs, how your body should align, and why those fundamentals matter.

What this chapter is here to teach you is how equitation actually functions in the show ring. How it reads from the middle. How details add up under pressure. How correctness, effectiveness, awareness, and presence work together when it matters most. Perfect position without understanding does not win classes. Functional equitation, ridden with intent, often does.

I was fortunate to learn early that fundamentals matter, and I learned them from the best. The photograph included in this chapter shows me at eight years old with Mrs. Crabtree herself. It isn't included for nostalgia. It's included because it represents the foundation beneath everything else in this book. Respect for the basics, paired with the ability to apply them in real time, in real competition.

This chapter assumes you care about equitation. It just refuses to pretend that perfection on paper is not always the same thing as winning in the ring.

WHAT JUDGES ARE ACTUALLY LOOKING FOR

Equitation is judged on the rider's position, effectiveness, form, and horsemanship skills.

The overall picture matters, but it's a picture made up of dozens of small decisions:

- Position: Are you functional, elegant, and effective, not stiff or over-posed?
- Horsemanship: Are you quietly and effectively influencing the horse?
- Overall Turnout: Are you polished, neat, and professionally presented?

The goal isn't to look like a mannequin. It's to ride with form and function in harmony, looking effortless, athletic, and in sync with your horse.

THE NON-NEGOTIABLES

There are certain standards in equitation that are not up for debate:

- Fit of Suit: Your suit must fit properly, not baggy, saggy, or stretched so tight you can barely move.
- Cleanliness of your attire
- Hair: Neat, tidy bun. No loose strands. No messy flyaways. No exceptions.

- Makeup: Understated and professional. You're riding, not auditioning for a music video.
- Functional Form: Non-Negotiable
- Expression: Pleasant, natural, connected. A pageant smile is not necessary.
- Horse-Rider Match: The horse should suit the rider's size and style for the cleanest overall picture.

In equitation, every detail speaks, even if you wish it didn't.

WALKING THE LINE AND WHY IT MATTERS

Riders awaiting the results of the Saddle Seat Equitation World Champion of Champions Class. Photo by Howard Schatzberg.

In Equitation classes judges are required to walk the lineup. And believe me, we look at everything from head to toe. And sometimes, that walk makes the difference between second and third...or even champion and reserve.

THE STORY THAT PROVES IT

I was judging a major national-level equitation class. First place was obvious. Second and third were extremely close. Both riders had beautiful patterns, effective horsemanship, and strong presence. When I walked the lineup, one rider had prepared her coat for the line up meticulously. The other, who easily could have been second, had overlooked one detail that kept pulling my eye: The flaps of her suit coat were flipped forward.

In equitation, we often pin or snap back the bottom corners of the coat to create a cleaner line along the rider's leg. In this case, the snaps were set too high, the flaps had flipped forward in the lineup, and the shiny silver snaps were glaringly obvious. And once I saw it, I couldn't unsee it. In a class that tight, where the rides were close enough to make it a true coin toss, that tiny detail literally cost her a reserve national championship title. This may seem harsh or unfair, but when everything else is even, presentation matters. Especially in equitation, where the rider's overall effect is the point.

LINEUP TIPS EVERY EQUITATION RIDER SHOULD KNOW

If you want to look like a serious, put-together contender in the lineup:

Adjust your suit coat immediately when you come into line.

- Do not sit on the flaps of your coat. Spread the back ones out evenly over the horse's hip. Fix the front coat flaps so they are turned back to show the shape of your leg. In fact, this was so ingrained in me when

I was young that I still do it in every single line up today.

Check your legs and posture, even while standing still.

- Stay tall, balanced, and correct. The lineup is still part of the class.

Keep a pleasant, neutral expression.

- Look present and confident, not frozen, forced, or performative.

Try to stay still and composed when the judge walks the line.

- No fidgeting, no shifting, no unnecessary adjustments.

Do not over-pose, stiffen up, or turn into a statue.

- You still need to ride your horse. Effective control matters more than looking artificially "perfect."

If your horse moves, quietly correct it.

- A soft "whoa" and a composed adjustment show real horsemanship. Overreacting does not nor does not doing anything at all.

Stay sharp until you leave the ring.

- Judges may be watching the entire time. Presentation should never go "off duty.".

PATTERN PERFORMANCE STARTS BEFORE THE PATTERN

Being great at patterns isn't just about execution, it's about preparation and professionalism before you even take your first step. If you're on deck, you need to be ready and fully prepared to begin the moment you're called. That said, don't crowd the rider before you.

One of the fastest ways to annoy management, staff, judges, and your fellow exhibitors is by holding up the class because you aren't ready to start your pattern when called. Stay respectfully off to the side until it's your turn, but be locked in and ready to go. Everyone, including show staff, is quietly timing these classes. Pattern classes already take longer than regular classes, and if you add unnecessary lag time by fumbling to get into the ring, you're not doing yourself (or the rest of the show) any favors.

Be ready. Be professional. Be efficient. It's one more detail that reflects your awareness, your horsemanship, and your respect for the ring.

HORSEMANSHIP OVER PERFECTION. WHAT JUDGES REALLY REWARD IN PATTERNS

In pattern work, mistakes happen at every level of competition. The trick isn't riding a perfect pattern.

It's riding through the imperfections like a professional. If you miss a transition, don't panic. If your horse gets tense, don't freeze or overcorrect. Stay on course. Execute the next segment. Many pattern classes, especially equitation classes, are scored in segments. That means a mistake in one part doesn't have to sink your whole ride…if you recover well. And often, how you recover is the very thing being judged.

THE HORSEMANSHIP MOVE THAT WON THE CLASS

I recently judged an Equitation Class with a set pattern. This class is weighted more heavily on the pattern and the final maneuver puts the rider right in front of the judge.

At that distance, we can see literally everything: Your control. Your cues. Your effectiveness. Your bond with your horse. In this class, two riders stood out, but they were very different. This made my job harder than expected, however in Equitation horsemanship should always prevail.

Therefore, the rider I chose as the winner displayed stellar skills, timing and an understanding of her horse during the pattern. When she trotted to me and stopped to back, the horse was very nervous. He resisted. Didn't want to back up. When she finished, he threatened to leap forward. Many riders would have panicked, clamped the reins, tighten up throughout their body and created more drama. She didn't. She opened three fingers on the rein, reached forward, and touched the back of her horse's neck. Then she quietly said, "Trot." The horse immediately relaxed. She held her hand there until he moved off softly, then closed her fingers and returned to the lineup like nothing happened. That single decision, done with total calm and tact, won her the class. In the biggest moment of pressure, she showed real horsemanship. And in equitation sometimes that matters more than perfection.

FINAL THOUGHT

Equitation rewards riders who respect the little things, who understand that how you ride is just as important as what you are riding. It's not always about having the fanciest horse. It's about how you prepare, how you recover, and how you carry yourself when the pressure is on.

Want to win in equitation? Then start treating the details like they're the deciding factor because sometimes, they are.

16

YES, THE JUDGING IS OVER, BUT...

You have ridden the ride, made your passes, survived the lineup, and heard the results. Maybe you are thrilled, maybe you are confused, or maybe you are furious. The part most people do not say out loud is what you do after the judging is over still matters. The card may be turned in, but the impression you leave does not stop there. The moments that follow can either solidify you as a respected competitor or quietly chip away at the reputation you are working so hard to build.

Judges notice how you carry yourself in the lineup. Trainers notice. Owners notice. Fellow riders and spectators notice. Even if it does not change a ribbon that day, your behavior contributes to your long-term opportunities, your barn's image, and the level of respect you earn in this sport. It also plays a big part in how much joy and fulfillment you actually get out of competing. This chapter is about what happens after the class, but make no mistake, it is still part of the show. Whether you are thrilled, disappointed, or somewhere in between, how you respond speaks volumes about your professionalism and character.

HOW YOU HANDLE THE RIBBON MATTERS

It is easy to forget that people are still watching after the results are called, but they are. How you respond to a ribbon, especially one you did not want, can either elevate your presence or undo the poise you just projected in the ring. Staring the judge down when you do not place as expected, storming out of the ring without taking your ribbon, or visibly showing anger during the lineup might feel justified in the moment, but it undercuts your professionalism and makes you look smaller, not stronger.

Being a good sport is not limited to the moments before you are judged. It extends from the way you enter the ring all the way to how you exit it, ribbon in hand. While your attitude should not affect your placing, your body language absolutely affects how you are perceived. Perception, fair or not, lingers. Riders who handle both wins and losses with grace build reputations that judges and peers respect and remember.

WHEN POST-CLASS BEHAVIOR GOES WRONG

Every judge, trainer, and seasoned spectator has seen the meltdown moments. There is the rider who rips the ribbon out of the ringmaster's hand and charges out of the ring. There is the rider who glares at the judge, rolls their eyes in lineup, or shakes their head dramatically. There is the rider who yanks on their horse's mouth in frustration after a call they do not agree with. There is even the rider who flat-out refuses the ribbon because they think they deserved better.

In those moments, it does not matter how good the ride was. That behavior becomes the story. That is what people remember, and it follows that rider from show to show. The sport is smaller than you think. Word travels and so does your reputation.

THE MOMENT I WILL NEVER FORGET

There is one post-class moment that has stayed with me for many years. At the time, I was not yet a judge, but I am now, and the rider involved still shows. She was a young rider at the time who ended up with last place. The ribbon was justified from my standpoint. She had picked up the wrong lead for a long time directly in front of the judge. There was a ring full of other viable entries in the class, which meant the outcome should not have been a mystery.

Instead of accepting the result, she made a choice I will never forget. She rode toward the out-gate as if she were going to collect her ribbon. Then she wheeled her horse around to face the judge's stand, took her hand off the rein, and shook it at the judge. It was not subtle, it was a deliberate and public act of disrespect. Then she turned and left the ring without the ribbon.

The judge, in my opinion, was generous, choosing not to write her up with the governing body of the show, even though it would have been justified. I have seen her display similar behavior in other instances, which tells me it was not a one-time lapse. It is a pattern and I still remember. If I ever end up judging her, will that memory keep her from winning if she clearly earns it? No. If she is the best in the class, she will get the blue ribbon. What would happen in a very close class, when every tiny impression can tip the scale, my guess is that human nature will come into play, but time will tell on this answer. What we do in the heat of the moment does not disappear just because the class is over. Sometimes it lingers for decades.

JUDGES HAVE LONG MEMORIES, BUT NOT ALWAYS PETTY ONES

Something that we don't like to admit or discuss is that judges are human. That being said, holding grudges and/or punishing people for past behavior should not come into play when marking the card. However, the brain absolutely stores a mental file labeled "this person handles pressure well" or "this rider becomes volatile when things go wrong." It is not personal. It is pattern recognition.

These impressions matter the most when the class is razor thin and the horses are closely matched. In those moments, grace under pressure reads as maturity and professionalism. Uncontrolled emotion reads as unpredictability. One rider looks steady. One rider looks like a gamble.

You are not being judged on your personality, but your demeanor communicates how trainable, coachable, and reliable you are. In a sport built on nuance, that matters more than most people realize.

WHAT TO DO WHEN YOU ARE FURIOUS OR HEARTBROKEN

Sometimes grace is not easy. You will have rides where the sting hits harder than you expected, where the result feels unfair or humiliating. You might feel like crying, yelling, or throwing something. That is normal. You are invested in this sport. It means you care. Big emotions do not make you weak. They make you human.

What separates serious competitors from everyone else is how they manage those emotions in public.

When you are furious or heartbroken, your first job is containment. You do not have to be happy, but you should stay in control. If you have to, bite the inside of your cheek. It sounds silly, but it interrupts the tears or the pout long enough to get you out of the ring with dignity. Pick a neutral point across the arena, a banner or a section of wall, and rest your eyes there so you are not glaring at the judge or scanning the crowd for sympathy.

No matter what happened in the ring, pat your horse. That pat is not for the judge or the audience. It is for your horse and for you. It reminds you that no ribbon erases the work you put in together. Sit up, take a breath, and ride out of the gate with as much composure as you can manage. Make yourself a simple rule. Hold it together until you are out of sight. Smile for a few strides. Keep your shoulders back. Exit like a professional.

Once you are back in the barn aisle or the tack stall, all bets are off. Cry. Stomp. Vent. Decompress however you need to. Protecting your professionalism in public does not mean denying your feelings. It means respecting the time and place to express them.

I learned this lesson early.

As a young equitation rider, I got beat a lot. And because equitation is judged entirely on the rider, I took those losses personally. Too personally, if I am being honest. To me, it did not just mean that I didn't win that day. It meant I was not good enough. Not talented enough. Not pretty enough on a horse. Not athletic enough. Not enough, period.

So yes, I left more than a few arenas on the verge of tears.

My dad understood something important long before I did. I was not ready to hear that my fears were not true. I was going to keep feeling them anyway. The issue was not my emotions. The issue was how they could be perceived. Not as heartbreak, but as poor sportsmanship, which was never what I intended.

So he made one rule. Cry all you want. Just wait until you get back to the barn and do it in the tack room.

I followed that rule for years. And eventually, I grew into the understanding that placing lower than first was not an attack on my worth, my future, or my entire life. It was simply one result on one day.

Judges notice the rider who can manage disappointment in the ring, in the lineup, and on the way out. That composure signals maturity, perspective, and long-term commitment. Learning when to hold it together and when to let it out is not about being tough. It is about growing up in the sport.

WINNING GRACEFULLY MATTERS TOO

Handling disappointment with professionalism is critical, but so is handling success with humility. Bad sportsmanship is not limited to riders who lose. We have all seen the other version. The over-the-top celebration while other riders are still sitting in the lineup. The smug looks. The exaggerated clapping. The loud "I knew it" or "finally" comments within earshot of the rest of the class.

Winning riders who forget their manners do just as much damage to their reputations, and sometimes more. You do not need to apologize for winning and by all means celebrate your wins, after all you earned them. You do need to respect the moment. Accept your ribbon with calm pride. Thank the ringmaster. Pat your horse. Smile in a way that matches the level of professionalism you want to be known for. Let your ride, not your reaction, be the story that people talk about later.

THE EXIT IS PART OF THE PERFORMANCE

Your ride does not necessarily end when the judge turns in the card. It ends when you exit the ring. That final stretch from the lineup to the out-gate is still part of the show. Your posture, your expression, and your interaction with your horse in those moments leave a lasting imprint. Think of it like finishing a performance routine. Skaters do not land their last jump and then slump off the ice. They finish with intention. Riders should do the same.

A clean, composed exit tells trainers, judges, and owners that you are steady, coachable, and emotionally mature. It tells your horse that you are still with them. Even if you are disappointed, you are still a team.

WHO IS WATCHING AND WHAT THEY REMEMBER

Do not assume that no one is paying attention after the class. Judges notice the rider who gives a soft pat to their horse after a tough trip. Trainers notice which riders they want to keep investing in. Owners notice which riders they might want to trust with a special horse in the future. Spectators talk. Word spreads about more than just who won. It spreads about who handled themselves like a professional and who did not.

Your behavior after a class is not just about pride in the moment. It is about future opportunities that you do not even know are being decided. You are always auditioning for something in this sport, whether you realize it or not.

FINAL THOUGHTS: PLAY THE LONG GAME

Your ride might be over, but your reputation walks out of the gate with you. Protect it like it matters, because it absolutely does. This sport rewards riders who think beyond today's ribbon. It rewards the ones who act like champions even on the days they do not win. In every lineup, every ribbon presentation, and every exit, you are building something that lasts longer than a single class. You are building a name people respect.

Ride hard. Compete honestly. Feel your feelings. But carry yourself in a way that your future self will be proud of. That is how you build a career and a legacy in this sport, not just a collection of multi-colored ribbons.

17

LOSING LOUDLY, LEARNING QUIETLY

If you show long enough, losing is not a possibility. It is a guarantee. The only question is how you handle it.

Judged competitions are not built for the emotionally fragile. You are choosing to be publicly evaluated while piloting a roughly thousand-pound animal with a mind of its own. If you want perfection, you picked the wrong sport and the wrong reality.

Loss is part of the job. It is not glamorous, in many cases it is not easy to swallow, and it is definitely not fun, but it is often the exact thing that shapes the riders who rise to the top. Some of your worst moments, the ones that hit your pride and make you question your direction, eventually become the same moments that sharpen your competitive edge.

THE TRUTH ABOUT LOSING

Most riders dread it, but every real competitor faces it. Losing is not an accident in this sport. It is inevitable. You put your training, your horse, and your ego on display. Sometimes you will come up short, and sometimes you will do it in front of a full house, your clients, your parents, and a judge who still does not know your name.

If you want to win at a high level, you have to be willing to lose first. The losses that matter are not the gentle ones. They are the ones that shake you enough to force you to level up. Every rider who looks polished and effortless has a history of bruised confidence behind them. Missed leads. Bad timing. Cards that did not go their way.

Winning is not built on charm or luck. It is built on resilience, reflection, and the refusal to let one bad class define you. Some riders take longer to find their stride. That does not make them weak. It makes them far more dangerous when their time finally comes.

If you are losing right now, that's okay. It means you are still in the fight. And if you're still in the fight, you can certainly figure out how to win it eventually. I think that is one of the most important qualities of fierce competitors, rebuilding after a disappointing class. It is especially hard when it's in public on a big stage. Recovering and coming back even better the next is not for the faint of heart or for the weak.

THE ART OF THE PUBLIC COMEBACK

Tiffany Wheeler winning the 2024 Five Gaited World Grand Championship with Midd's Delaney for owner Christine Broder. Photo by Doug Shiftlet.

At the highest level of competition, even exceptional partnerships experience moments that do not go exactly as planned. What separates the best is not perfection, but the ability to respond with poise, confidence, and professionalism in very public settings. A great example of this came in 2024 with Tiffany Wheeler and Midd's Delaney at the World Grand Championship Horse Show.

On Tuesday night, the pair competed in the Five-Gaited Mare Stake. The class did not unfold the way Tiffany had planned, and she left the ring without a ribbon. Moments like this happen, even at the very highest level. What matters most is not the outcome, but the response.

From an outsider's perspective, the way Tiffany Wheeler handled the days that followed was not only admirable, but instructive. She did not lose belief in her horse or herself. She remained composed, evaluated the situation honestly, and made thoughtful adjustments on a tight timeline, all under the pressure of the sport's biggest stage. Just as importantly, she demonstrated a deep understanding of how to navigate both the highs and lows of this sport, focusing on what truly mattered and putting it into action. There is much to learn from Tiffany in general, and this particular journey to the World Grand Championship is no exception.

Just 24 hours later, Tiffany and Delaney returned to the ring and put those adjustments to the test, winning a very deep Ladies Mare class with a ride that was confident, composed, and polished. Only three days after that, she delivered one of the most meaningful wins in our industry, becoming one of only five women to win the Five-Gaited World Championship, against a field that represented some of the greatest horses of our time.

In the span of five days, Tiffany and Delaney moved from a disappointing moment to earning the ultimate reward in our sport. Not by forcing a comeback, but by staying steady, focused, and firmly committed to belief in the horse, herself, and the process.

That is what a professional comeback looks like. It is not about erasing a moment or proving anything to anyone. It is about showing up again with clarity, confidence, and trust. When that mindset is paired with preparation, the results often take care of themselves.

Here, Tiffany shares what that week required mentally and emotionally, and how she approached returning to the ring with confidence while the spotlight was still very much on her.

IN TIFFANY'S WORDS

It's no secret that Delaney was a fractious mare. She was 8 years old the first time she entered the show ring in Spring of 2024. After a strong show at Rock Creek, it became evident that she may be a Louisville contender, so I started looking in that direction. I'd entered her in both the Mare Stake, along with the Ladies Mare class, because you never know....

And as it turns out, I'm so glad I did. I knew Louisville would be a lot for this mare, quite possibly too much for the stage she was at. Anyone who's ever shown in Freedom Hall knows how bright and loud center ring is. From the cheering audience to the people screaming on the rail, to the music over the loudspeakers, then add in the thundering of hooves around you, it's a lot for any horse. It's intense. Nothing prepares you for it, nor is there any way to prepare your horse for it. They just have to experience it.

Delaney warmed up for the Mare Stake as she always did... very unimpressive. But that's how she needed to be. Because before long, she'd be crawling out of her skin. As soon as I was down the ramp into Freedom Hall, I knew I was in trouble. She was absolutely star struck, gawking at the rail, trembling at the loud music, and then a herd of horses passed her. She immediately slipped into her slow gait and that was it. I never got her to trot the first direction. Luckily, I was one of the last ones to enter the ring, so we ambled our way down to the far end, where I continued in small circles trying to get her to pick up her trot, and more importantly, trying to stay out of everyone's way and not mess them up. They soon called for the walk. Again, luckily, I came in almost last, so that nightmare was over fairly soon. As she slow gaited and racked, I could feel her confidence building and by the second direction, she was settled in and working great. But it was too late. Unfortunately, you have to perform ALL of your gaits to earn a ribbon. The one judge who did NOT see us not trot did tie us first, but the other two judges had me off their cards, and rightfully so. But I'll never forget the crowd cheering for us as we left the ring. They could see what she was.

To say I was devastated was an understatement. I told both Chris Broder and Steve that it was all just too much for her and

I'd asked too much too soon. I had dozens of people coming to me telling me how fabulous she was, but I was completely dejected. I went home that night to lick my wounds.

The next morning (3:30 am) we were up working horses, and I had something to ride in Freedom Hall. The day I'd taken Delaney up there to work before she showed, the lights were off in there. I'd never seen that before, but when she worked it was quite dark in there. That next morning, all the lights were on and it was bright as could be. I immediately asked her groom to get her ready to ride again, changed her bridle (again), and rode her up to Freedom Hall to work under the bright lights and she was perfection. That's when I made the decision to show her that night in the Ladies Class. I couldn't replicate all the loud noise of Freedom Hall that morning, but at least she could SEE what she was getting ready to trot in to.

That night I trotted down Freedom Hall even more conservatively than usual. I didn't care WHAT our first direction trot looked like, just so long as we trotted. And she did. Once that first trot was out of the way, she was ready to roll and won the class unanimously.

So, the lesson of this story is...no matter how badly a ride goes, the only thing you can control is your reaction to it. You have to dig deep and no trainer, spouse, friend or anyone else can help you do that. YOU have to have that internal dialogue with yourself. YOU have to have the willpower, fortitude and the willingness to try (and possibly fail) again. But I'd always rather lose trying than to not lose at all.

THE RIDE AND THE LOSS THAT STILL LIVES ON YOUTUBE

GoPro View of Freedom Hall. Beauty Marc & Allison Deardorff. Photo is from National Horseman's GoPro footage.

I have lost a lot over the course of my show ring career and I am sure I will lose even more before it's over. Some losses are louder than others in my mind. In fact, I still think about the year I wore a GoPro in one of the Kentucky County Fair Championships at Louisville. The best and worst part of this loss is that I get to continue to lose publicly on YouTube. As I write this, there are currently more than 16,000 views on the video.

But I digress, back to the story. It was a clean ride on a top quality and very talented horse, but clearly something felt short and I ended up third with a 1-2-3. Leaving with my yellow ribbon, I felt like I had let the whole world down including my horse, the owner, The National Horseman Magazine (who had asked me to wear the GoPro), my dad, my staff, everyone who had a part in getting me and the horse into the ring that night. And let me tell you, nothing humbles you like walking down Stopher Walk in disappointment with a camera strapped to your chest while you try to sound composed on the audio, knowing every sigh coupled with awkward silence is about to become public record.

Now that I have had a few years to recover, I would love another chance to wear that GoPro and deliver the ride that The National Horseman hoped for. Maybe Allison Lambert will help me out with that someday.

WHERE RIDERS GET STUCK

You can tell who is going to rise and last in this sport by how they handle disappointment.

Some riders blame the judge every single time and never look inward. That mindset feels protective, but it is a dead end. If the problem is always external, there is nothing to fix. Growth requires ownership, even when the judging feels unfair.

Some riders spiral and shrink. They take one bad class as proof that they are not good enough and start riding smaller to avoid standing out. That approach feels safer in the moment, but it quietly erodes confidence and presence.

Others get scared of losing again and start riding cautiously. Riding cautiously is not the same as riding correctly. Safe riding removes risk, but it also removes impact. In a competitive class, safety reads as hesitation. And hesitation is forgettable.

This is where most riders plateau. The riders who move forward do something different. They separate emotion from evaluation. They let themselves feel disappointed, but they do not let that disappointment drive the next decision. They go back to the barn and ask better questions. Was my strategy right for this class? Did I commit when it mattered? Did I ride the horse I brought in, or the horse I wished I had?

If you want to win, you must be willing to lose publicly and learn privately. Public loss is part of the deal. What matters is what you do with it when no one is watching.

Evaluation is not self-criticism. It is self-respect. It is the willingness to be honest about habits, preparation, and choices. Riders who skip that step are not truly competing, they are just hoping.

Hope is passive. Strategy is active. One keeps you stuck. The other moves you forward.

THE BOUNCE BACK BLUEPRINT

This is how I rebuild.

- **Step 1: Feel it. Own It.**

I do not cry in or out of the tack room when I lose anymore, but I get quiet. I replay everything. Training choices, prep, shoeing, fitness (my own and my horse's), timing. Not to punish myself but to understand.

- **Step 2: Watch the video**

I hate watching myself show, but I do it anyway. The footage always tells the truth. Did I miss a moment? Did I blend in? Was I proactive or reactive? You cannot fix anything you refuse to look at.

- **Step 3: Adjust the plan**

Sometimes the fix is small. Sometimes it is a full reset. My biggest breakthroughs have come after classes I did not win.

- **Step 4: Experiment at the right shows**

I take risks or try new strategies or divisions at smaller shows, not on the biggest stages (though sometimes this is unavoidable). If there is a new strategy or timing I want to test, I try to do it when the stakes are lower.

- **Step 5: Show up again**

Showing up again is what separates contenders from tourists. I enter into every ring believing I can win, not because I am naive, but because I have seen too many classes swing in unexpected ways and I have to believe it can swing my way, because that belief is what keeps me coming back for more.

DELUSION OR DETERMINATION

Delusional confidence matters. It keeps you in the game.

Even when I understand exactly why I did not win, I still believe I can fix it and come back stronger. That mindset has saved me more times than I can count. In this sport we often have to grow while people watch. Clients, critics, judges. There is no hiding.

Some of my best rides were comeback rides. Not because I changed who I was, but because I refused to disappear. Staying in the fight eventually changes the way people talk about you.

WHAT MAKES A TRUE COMPETITOR

It is not the perfect ride. It is not the victory pass. It is how you walk down Stopher Walk with a third place ribbon and a camera on your vest and still believe the next round is within reach.

It is watching the footage and saying, "Alright. We can fix this." It is showing up even when your confidence is cracked but not broken. Losing does not take you out of the running for greatness but quitting definitely does.

18

PRESENTATION AND PREPARATION ARE PART OF THE PERFORMANCE

Allison at age 3 with her father, Don Deardorff. Clean boots are a must even in leadline.

First impressions matter more than most exhibitors realize. There is a simple truth that judges rarely say out loud but think constantly: if you did not care enough to shine your boots, what else did you not care about. Before you even trot through the gate, you have already communicated a clear message. From the shine of your horse's coat to the shape of your derby, every detail tells us something about your preparation, your pride, your discipline, and the level of respect you have for the horse who is carrying you into the ring. These things matter, not because judges are looking for a reason to criticize, but because your turnout is the visible evidence of how seriously you take the sport. Sloppy presentation does not just make you look disorganized, it pulls attention away from your horse, and that is the real problem. In the show ring, you are not the painting, you are the frame, your job is to showcase the horse, not distract from them with a falling-out bun or a neon glitter browband that blinds half the warm-up ring before you even enter.

RIDER PRESENTATION: CONFIDENCE IN THE DETAILS

Rider turnout begins long before your horse takes a single step, and it is one of the clearest indicators of mindset. Horse shows can start early, they are often stressful, and the glamour wears off quickly, but nothing says "I do not really believe I can win" like showing up looking like you got dressed in the parking lot (though I am sure that many of us have had to do this on occasion.) Hair is often the first giveaway. If your bun slides down your neck before the first trot, judges notice, and once we notice, it becomes impossible not to notice. Your bun does not need to be glamorous or sparkly, but it does need to be secure. Learn how to do your bun properly or designate someone who can do it for you. You do not want to march into the gate dropping bobby pins like breadcrumbs, only to end up with a photo you need to Photoshop because half your hair escaped during your best pass.

The same level of intention applies to your headgear. An unshaped derby or unsmoothed top hat takes you from elegant competitor to someone who pulled a costume piece from the trunk and hoped it would pass. Get your hats professionally shaped and cleaned, this is non-negotiable. Transport them in an actual hat box. Treat them like part of your competitive equipment, not afterthoughts.

Suit fit tells us even more. A well-tailored off-the-rack suit will always beat an expensive one that fits like a tarp. Fit matters more than the brand, and a rider who invests in proper tailoring looks prepared, streamlined, and confident. Cleanliness is another non-negotiable. Dirty boots, dusty gloves, and mud-spattered coats do not say you were busy. They say you did not believe the details mattered.

When two rides are close, those details absolutely matter. Your expression matters too. A dead-eyed hostage stare communicates nerves and disconnect. A forced pageant smile looks equally manufactured. Judges appreciate a pleasant, present expression that shows confidence without theatrics.

Style is welcome, but subtlety wins. Your personality can shine through color choices and tasteful sparkle, but your horse must remain the focal point. If your jacket is louder than your trot, your priorities are off. Presentation is not about being overly flashy or pretty. It is about being intentional.

BACK NUMBERS: VISIBILITY MATTERS

Riders await the results at The Morgan Grand National and World Championship Horse Show.

Back numbers may seem like a small detail, but they play a significant role in the judging process. Quite simply, if a judge cannot clearly see an exhibitor's number, it becomes difficult to accurately record that performance. Most judges genuinely want to reward strong rides and good presentations, but that can only happen when identification is clear and immediate.

In fast-moving classes, missing or obscured numbers create unnecessary challenges. When a number is not visible, judges or ringmasters may be forced to divert attention away from evaluating performance in order to identify an exhibitor. This can mean leaning to see behind a rider or driver, asking the announcer for clarification, or walking in from the center of the ring to confirm a number. These moments interrupt the flow of judging and do not benefit the exhibitor.

For drivers, numbers are often hidden by coat tails draped over the seat, jackets hanging too loosely, or blouses that cover the number entirely. Riders encounter different but equally common issues. Numbers that are over-trimmed can be difficult to read, particularly when the white border is cut too close to the printed digits. Without sufficient contrast, the numbers can visually blend into dark coats or dark riding attire, which most exhibitors wear, making it hard to distinguish between similar digits from the center of the ring.

Placement also matters. Numbers positioned too high, too low, off-center, or at an angle are harder to identify quickly. When a number sits on a curved or uneven part of the back, it can catch arena lighting in a way that creates glare or shadowing, making the digits difficult or impossible to read. For this reason, the number should be placed on the flattest part of the exhibitor's back, centered between the shoulder blades, where it can lie straight and remain consistently visible despite movement and lighting.

Equally important is how the number is secured. Numbers that are not fastened at all corners can flap, fold, or shift during a class. Magnets placed inconsistently or too close to the digits can distort the shape of the number and further reduce readability. Using magnets or pins on all four corners helps keep the number flat, stable, and legible throughout the class.

In a competitive environment, details matter. Your back number should support your presentation, not detract from it. Making it easy for the judge to identify you allows the focus to remain on your performance without unnecessary distractions that could easily be avoided.

YOUR VOICE IS PART OF THE PICTURE

Your voice is part of your presentation whether you like it or not. A quiet, well-timed "walk" or "easy" can elevate a performance because it demonstrates partnership and finesse, but when your voice becomes the background soundtrack of the entire class, it shifts from supportive to distracting. There is a difference between a soft "good boy" that only your horse hears and a panicked shout of "CANTER, CANTER, WHOA" that echoes across the arena. One sounds polished. The other sounds frantic. Subtle wins. Shouting does not. Use your voice with intention, the same way you would use your hands or seat. Everything you do should complement your presentation, not compete with it.

TACK, VEHICLES, AND EQUIPMENT: THE DEVIL IS IN THE DETAILS

Your equipment speaks just as loudly as your suit. Dirty tack is a clear sign of rushing, disorganization, or a lack of respect for the class. If I can see grime from the center of the ring, you did not clean your tack, you ran a damp rag across it and hoped for magic. Or worse, yet did nothing at all. Every piece of tack should be intentional and appropriate. It does not need to be expensive. It simply needs to be clean, safe, and show-ready.

Since we are talking about details, here is a story. I have a good friend who regularly judges major shows and is genuinely obsessed with one thing: polished brass Freedman bridle emblems. He notices them every time, especially when riders pass too close or during a lineup. If that brass is dull or dirty, he remembers. In a tough class, when two rides are almost identical, that detail can tip the balance. It may sound extreme, but it is true. At the highest levels, small differences become deciding factors.

Your browband is another area where riders often try too hard. The goal is elegant, not flashing a neon sign on the Vegas Strip. Stick with traditional browband colors and styles for your discipline. Leave the glitter, rhinestones, neon vinyl, and craft-store experiments at home. Browbands should highlight your horse's face, not compete with it.

Equipment safety matters as much as appearance. If your

cart rattles so loudly it sounds like you are delivering lumber, or your bike tire goes flat mid-class, you are not just distracting the judge, you are creating risk. Of course, judges understand that accidents can happen and sometimes equipment failure is unavoidable, but doing your due diligence before the class will significantly cut down on the risk. Check your stitching, check your harnesses, check all of your wheels. A few minutes of care can save your class and sometimes your safety.

HORSE TURNOUT: RESPECT STARTS HERE

You do not need the most expensive horse in the division to win. You do need to show that you respect the horse you have. A properly conditioned horse, clipped cleanly, groomed thoroughly, and presented with pride communicates something powerful. A dusty coat, uneven clip job, or an unbrushed tail all tell a very different story. They say you ran out of time, you misjudged your preparation, or you thought small details would not matter. Clean hooves, brushed tails, freshly clipped points, and shiny coats show us that you understand this is a formal sport and that you value your horse's presentation as much as your own.

WHEN CLEAN FEET WIN A CHAMPIONSHIP

Years ago, at a small show, one of our riders won a tight championship. The class had five comparable horses, and nothing about their conformation, movement or manners separated them clearly. When they lined up, I saw the judge walk the line and stare at the horses' feet as he backed them. It seemed odd, but I did not question it. After the class, he approached me and said, "Do you know why I chose your horse to win that class?" I said no. His answer was simple. "Your horse's feet were the only ones that looked prepared." That detail, something we had always treated as standard, made the difference. Clean feet did not make our horse better, but they made the choice easier. In a tight class, those tiny details become tiebreakers.

Turnout is not about money. It is about care, effort, and pride. It is something you can control every single time you show.

WHY IT MAKES A DIFFERENCE

Turnout is not about impressing the judge with how much you spent. It is about presenting yourself and your horse with respect, pride, and professionalism. It sends a message that you take this seriously and that you honor the animal who is carrying you into the ring. When you show up put together, prepared, and intentional, you do more than influence a judge's perception. You transform your own and you start to see yourself as a competitor who deserves to win before the ribbons are even called. Your performance begins the moment you step through the gate. Show up like someone who belongs in that ring. Show up like someone who is building a winning career, not just entering another class.

CARE FIRST, COMPETE SECOND

One of the fastest ways to not only annoy the judge, but also frustrate your trainer, veterinarian, farrier, chiropractor, and anyone else invested in your horse's well-being is to neglect what your horse actually needs.

Skipping routine vet work. Stretching farrier cycles too long. Ignoring soreness because the horse is "still usable." Hauling a horse to a show that is "just a little off" and hoping adrenaline will cover it. None of this is dedication. It is unfair and quite frankly, it's selfish.

These horses are athletes. And unlike human athletes, they

cannot tell us exactly what hurts, where it hurts, or how long it has been building. That responsibility belongs entirely to the humans involved.

Care is not optional. It is foundational. Judges see the results of care long before we ever see a ribbon. We see condition, soundness, muscle tone, balance, and willingness. We see horses that are comfortable in their body and horses that are compensating. No amount of talent can hide discomfort for long. Poor care shows up as resistance, irregularity, tension, or inconsistency. Riders often blame training or attitude when the real issue is physical management that has been ignored or delayed.

There is also a professionalism component some riders overlook. When care is inconsistent, trainers are forced into damage control instead of development. Vets and farriers are put in reactive positions instead of preventive ones. Horses end up being asked to perform through discomfort instead of being supported through it. That is not how successful programs are built.

Actionable reality check:

- Vet work should be routine, not emergency-based
- Farrier schedules should be proactive, not reactive
- Body work should be maintenance, not crisis management

If your horse is telling you something is off, believe them. Rest is part of training. Even bodybuilders program recovery as aggressively as workouts. Prevention is cheaper than repair.

Here is some honest tough love. If you say you cannot afford proper care, or you do not believe in it, this may not be the right sport for you at this time. That is not judgment. That is the reality of it. Horses require ongoing investment to be shown ethically and competitively. Care first. Competition second. Everything else follows.

WHAT ABOUT PAID ADVERTISING?

This is one of the questions I get asked most often. How important is it to advertise in show horse publications? Here is my honest answer: it is not required nor is it necessary.

Speaking from the judge's perspective, I do not need a magazine to tell me if I like a certain horse. I do not care if I have never seen your name in print, online, or anywhere else. When a horse trots into the ring and takes my breath away, that is what has my attention. I can spot a great horse in a crowded class, buried on the rail, or coming from a program I have never heard of. If a horse is exceptional, I will find it. That has always been true.

Great horses are everything to me, and for that reason alone, advertising is not a requirement for success in the show ring.

That does not mean advertising has no value. It simply means it is often misunderstood. Advertising is not a shortcut, and it is certainly not a guarantee. What it can do, when done well, is create familiarity. A well-executed, high-quality, and consistent advertising presence helps a judge recognize you more quickly when you enter the ring. That recognition can shorten the time it takes us to assess what we are seeing. Familiarity does not win a class, but it can slightly warm the lens through which a performance is viewed, and that recognition generally works in your favor rather than against you.

The reality, however, is that consistency is expensive. Unless you have an unlimited budget, maintaining constant visibility is simply not realistic for most exhibitors. That does not mean advertising should be avoided. It means it should be approached intentionally.

If you have the funds to advertise, do it with purpose. Advertise your major wins. Promote thoughtfully in the lead-up to important shows. Use design and messaging that reflect the quality of your horse and your program. You do not need to be everywhere, all the time, to be effective.

I also want to be clear about my respect for horse publications. I genuinely love them and always have. As a horse-obsessed kid, I collected magazines, cut out photos of my favorite horses and riders, and made scrapbooks to study, admire, and learn from. Today, I encourage my clients to advertise, and I enjoy seeing their photos in print as much as they do. These publications play an important role in our industry by promoting the sport, telling its stories, and supporting the people who make it run. Many have been incredibly supportive of me, my family, and my program over the years, and I am deeply grateful for that. However, when it comes to judging, advertising does not influence my decisions.

Judges are there to evaluate what they see in the ring, in real time. They are not placing horses based on what appeared in a magazine last month, what arrived in an email blast, or what circulated on social media. Advertising does not replace quality, preparation, or execution, and it does not override what happens between the in-gate and the lineup.

Advertising has evolved, however, and it is worth acknowledging that reality. Most publications now include digital exposure alongside print, and I will be honest: I truly do open and read most of the email blasts that come into my inbox. I may not linger on each one, but I see them. A sharp, well-designed ad that appears shortly before a major show can create recognition, and that familiarity may help a judge connect the dots more quickly when you trot into the ring.

Even with that said, advertising should never be your strategy for winning. If you choose to advertise, do so because it aligns with your goals and your budget, not because you believe it is required to be taken seriously. Advertise your wins. Promote selectively before major shows. Avoid going broke trying to stay visible. And do not let anyone convince you that a full-page ad is the price of credibility.

If your horse is the best in class and you ride it well, we will find you.

SOCIAL MEDIA: VISIBILITY WITHOUT LOSING CONTROL

Social media has become part of the modern show horse world, whether you participate actively or not. Used wisely, it can support your visibility as a serious competitor, help showcase your horse, and contribute positively to your reputation. Used carelessly, it can do the opposite.

Everything you post contributes to how you are perceived. That includes judges, trainers, owners, and peers. Social media does not exist in a vacuum. It is part of your overall presentation, and your reputation travels faster online than it ever did through word of mouth.

If you choose to use social media, be intentional. Post positive images of your horse. Choose photos that reflect quality, preparation, and professionalism. If you are unsure which images to share, ask your trainer to help you select the best photos from the class, the warm-up, or even the barn aisle. A quiet, special moment often tells a better story than an over-edited highlight or an emotional reaction.

Avoid posting images that undermine the impression you are trying to create. Poor moments, awkward expressions, unflattering angles, or visible tension rarely serve you or your horse. Neither do public complaints, frustration, or commentary that invites speculation. What feels harmless in the moment can linger far longer than intended.

Social media can be a powerful tool for visibility, particularly if you are building a farm, breeding program, or long-term presence in the horse show world. In those cases, working with a social media professional can be a smart investment. There are many knowledgeable experts who understand branding, storytelling, and audience perception, and their guidance can help you avoid common mistakes.

That said, social media is optional. Much like advertising in publications, it should only be part of your strategy if it matters to you. You do not need to post constantly to be taken seriously. You do not need to document every class or every ribbon. And you do not need an online presence to earn respect in the show ring.

What matters most is that whatever you put out into the world aligns with the reputation you want to build. If you choose to use social media, use it thoughtfully, professionally, and with restraint. If you choose not to use it, that is equally valid.

Visibility is a tool, not a requirement. Reputation, however, is always in play.

19

BEYOND THE RIBBON. RIDING FOR MORE

There is a certain energy that separates winning rides from the rest of the class, and it is not always attached to the fanciest horse or the rider from the biggest barn. It is the presence of someone who shows up like they belong in the winner's circle. Someone who rides with the quiet belief that they can win, even when the odds do not look like they are in their favor.

This chapter is about riding like that person. Especially on the days when the frontrunners do not bring their best.

BE READY TO STEP UP WHEN THE FAVORITES SLIP

Let's be honest. Sometimes you know you are not sitting on the fanciest horse in the class. Maybe your horse does not have the biggest motion, the longest resume, or the most expensive price tag. That reality can be hard to ignore when you trot through the gate.

That being said, even the best horses and the most seasoned riders have off days. Mistakes happen, energy drops, timing gets slightly off and when that moment comes, the judge is actively looking for someone else to step into the top spot. Be that rider.

Too often, competitors decide they cannot win simply because of who else is in the ring. They coast through the class doing a respectable job, but not an exceptional one. Meanwhile, the so-called unbeatable entry has a misstep or gives a lackluster ride, and instead of capitalizing, everyone else plays it safe. The judge is left with no clear alternative.

Do not fall into that trap. Show like you can beat the best, because sometimes you will. And once you do, it becomes easier to do it again.

Judges remember who stepped up when the opportunity was there. You begin to build momentum, credibility, and a reputation for being the rider who can deliver when it counts. The next time you are in the ring with that same top horse or rider, you are no longer just the underdog. You are the one they know can make it interesting.

Classes are not supposed to be awarded based on potential or price tags. They are awarded based on what happens in that moment. Be ready when the moment is yours, and make sure they remember you the next time.

THE TURNING POINT YOU MIGHT NEVER SEE

Most classes have a turning point. Sometimes it is obvious, like a break or a wrong lead. Other times it is subtle. A rider hesitates for a stride. A horse loses animation. A correction comes a second too late. You may never see that moment from your position in the ring, but the judge does.

This is the reason why you should never coast. You never assume the class is over, never decide someone else has already won. Until the judge turns in their card, everything is still in play. Classes turn on inches, not miles. They turn on moments, not minutes. Your job is to stay engaged, present, and competitive from the first stride to the very last one.

When you feel the panic rise mid-class, when the thought creeps in that it is already over, I want you to hear this clearly: it is not. Not yet.

If you can hold it together and finish strong, you may be the rider who edges out a mistake you never even knew your competition made. That is how close this sport gets and that is why presence matters so much. It is also why I coach and ride as if every class is winnable until the final stride.

WHEN NO ONE WANTS TO WIN

Early in my judging career, I was judging a predominantly Saddlebred show. One of the classes that day was an Open English Pleasure class, open to all breeds. The entries were mostly Saddlebreds, with a few Morgans, an Arabian or two, and a Friesian. Fourteen horses entered the ring. Believe me when I say, it was literally like judging apples and oranges and not a single one came in like a winner. I hesitate to use the word mediocre, because it can sound dismissive, but it's the most accurate way to describe what I was seeing. There was nothing glaringly wrong with the class, but there was also nothing exceptional. No horse distinguished itself through presence, consistency, or execution. Judges will tell you that these are often the hardest classes to judge. As the class went on, the problem became clearer. Every single horse made a mistake. Some were more obvious than others, but most were minor bobbles: a transition that wasn't quite clean, a loss of balance, a moment of tension. No one imploded. But no one rose to the occasion either. That was the issue. No horse was bad enough to clearly deserve last. No horse was strong enough to clearly deserve first. Up until that point, judging had felt fairly seamless to me. I've always been able to organize my notes, keep track of numbers, prioritize the specifications of the class, and make decisions efficiently. I've always trusted my eye. I've always trusted my process. However, at that moment, I felt pressure. I couldn't draw the class out any longer and nothing was changing. The ringmaster was waiting. It was time to call for the lineup, and I had no clear winner and no clear loser. The truth is, I could have assigned placings almost arbitrarily. In a class like that, very few people would have challenged the result. I could have shuffled numbers, turned in my card, and moved on. Instead, I made a conscious decision to treat the moment as a learning experience. I knew there would be other classes like this in my judging career, and I needed a way to handle them honestly and consistently. If performance alone wasn't separating the horses, then I needed another legitimate way to do my job. So I decided to default to quality. I've told a story elsewhere in this book about a judge choosing a winner based on feet. In this class, I placed the horses based on overall quality and turnout. I asked myself a simple question: If everything else is equal, which horse would I most want to take home? That meant quality of horse, suitability to the division, correctness of type, and overall presentation. It wasn't about flash or favoritism. It was about making a thoughtful distinction when the class itself refused to provide one. It's no secret that I tend to default to quality when I judge. I've been called out on it before. However, when execution, consistency, and performance are effectively equal, a judge still has an obligation to sort the class. Something has to matter, something has to separate them when everything else is equal. That class taught me two important lessons. First, situations like this are far more common than exhibitors realize. Judges are not always handed an obvious winner. Second, when riders show up trying not to lose instead of riding to win, they often create exactly this kind of class. When everyone plays it safe and everyone avoids risk, the judge is left to place horses based on details most exhibitors never realize are quietly in play. If you want to avoid being decided by a tiebreaker you didn't even know existed, you have to give the judge something to reward.

HOW TO CARRY MOMENTUM INTO FUTURE CLASSES

Once you have had that breakthrough moment, once you have beaten the big name, the World Champion, or the high-dollar horse, you have entered a different category. Do not downplay it. Do not second-guess it. Build on it.

Do not change what worked. Stay grounded in the habits and preparation that got you there. Treat the next class like a continuation, not a reset. Ride as if you are picking up where you left off and expect to be noticed. Judges will be watching to see if your win was a fluke or the beginning of a pattern. Show them the consistency they are looking for.

Protect your energy and do not let whispers from the stands or sudden attention pull you off your routine. Recognition is earned by staying composed, not by chasing the spotlight. Breakthrough wins are not just about one ribbon. They are the beginning of a shift in how you are seen, and just as importantly, in how you see yourself.

WHAT JUDGES ACTUALLY REMEMBER

Many riders assume judges only remember the best horses, the biggest barns, or the most dramatic mistakes. That is simply not true.

Judges remember the rider who showed up to win when no one expected it. They remember the team that showed clear improvement since the last time they competed. They remember the comeback ride, the confident performance after a rough class or a tough season. They remember the rider who stepped into a deep, competitive class and gave them a real decision to make.

When you beat a favorite fair and square, the judge takes notice. The next time you enter the ring, you are evaluated with more attention, tighter comparisons, and more consideration in close calls. That is how reputations are built. Not just by winning, but by winning when it matters.

WHY YOU'RE REALLY HERE

At some point, every rider has to confront an uncomfortable question. What outcome are you actually chasing when you trot through the in-gate?

For some riders, the ribbon is the goal. For others, it is validation, recognition, or proof that they belong. And for another group, the ribbon is simply feedback. Judges can feel the difference.

When a rider is riding for approval, it shows in their posture, their urgency, and their reactions. When a rider is riding for mastery, it shows in their calm, their patience, and their decision-making. One approach tightens the horse. The other allows the horse to work.

Judges are not blind to motivation. Riders who show up focused on improvement tend to ride cleaner, manage mistakes better, and leave the ring with credibility, regardless of the placing. Riders who show up desperate for validation often leave frustrated, even when they win.

If your only measure of success is a ribbon, you will eventually resent the process. If your measure of success includes growth, skill, and consistency, the ribbons tend to follow. Judges respect riders who understand the difference.

HANDLING THE PRESSURE

Pressure is everywhere in this sport.

From your trainer:

- Your trainer might be intense. Most successful ones are. That intensity comes from how much we care. We have poured our lives into this work, and we want to see you succeed. If you are overwhelmed by this, you need to speak up. The strongest coach-athlete relationships are built on communication and mutual respect.

From your competitors:

- Deep classes bring heat. Your job is not to out-pressure anyone. It is to out-focus them. You do not need to beat everyone. You need to show your best, and more often than not, that is what wins.

From yourself:

- This is often the hardest pressure to manage. Inner critics, doubt, and perfectionism creep in quickly. Learn to replace that voice with a better one. Try telling yourself, "I am prepared," or "I belong here," before you trot in. That is not fake confidence. It is a decision.

WHEN YOU ARE THE FAVORITE

Pressure does not disappear when you become the one to beat. If anything, it becomes more precise, more visible, and more personal.

Every owner wants to win, whether their horse cost $750,000 or $7,500. Talent and investment can raise expectations, but they do not change the fundamentals of competition. It is often easier to win with the more expensive, better-bred, better-prepared horse. What is not easier is managing the pressure that comes with it.

Being the favorite does not make a win automatic. It simply raises the volume of expectation. When you do not win with the horse everyone assumed would take the class, the disappointment feels sharper. Not just because of the result, but because of the narrative around it. People notice. You notice. The weight of that expectation is real, and pretending otherwise does not help.

The pressure itself is not the problem. Pressure is internal. It is created by how much meaning you assign to the outcome. Riders who struggle as favorites are not being beaten by the competition. They are being beaten by their own urgency to justify the label.

The solution is not to spiral or overcorrect. It is to narrow your focus back to the work. Ride the class in front of you. Execute the fundamentals. Let go of the storyline and stay inside the process. Favorites lose when they start riding to protect a reputation instead of riding to perform.

The strongest competitors understand this. They accept the expectation without letting it control them. They learn from losses without attaching them to identity. And when they win again, it is not because they were supposed to. It is because they stayed disciplined enough to earn it.

PEOPLE OVER PLACINGS

Some of the best memories you will take from a horse show will have nothing to do with ribbons. They come from the quiet mornings in the barn, the laughter in the grooming aisle, the inside jokes that carry you through a long season, and the moments you spend cheering for someone else's success.

This sport is demanding. The hours are long. The investment is significant. The pressure is real. Without camaraderie, it becomes isolating very quickly.

Camaraderie is not accidental. It is a choice you make every day at the show. You can want to win and still be gracious. You can be competitive and still clap for another rider. You can be focused on your own goals without treating everyone else like an obstacle. The riders who manage this balance tend to last longer in the sport and enjoy it more while they are in it.

Connection matters for more than morale. Supportive environments create better riders. They allow people to take risks, recover from losses, and stay grounded during wins. They remind you that one class does not define your worth and that success in this sport is built over time, not decided by a single ribbon.

Judges notice this culture as well. We see barns that support each other and barns that fracture under pressure. We see riders who acknowledge others and riders who isolate themselves. While placings are based on performance, professionalism and presence always leave an impression.

Be the rider who contributes to the atmosphere, not drains it. Celebrate your barn mates. Support the riders around you. Protect the culture of the sport you love. Placings fade, but people stay. And the energy you bring into the barn aisle has a way of finding its way back to you.

THE BURNOUT CHECK-IN

Burnout in this sport rarely shows up all at once. It creeps in quietly. You start dreading show mornings. You feel flat after rides that used to excite you. You question your place, your progress, or whether the effort is worth it.

When that happens, pause and ask yourself a few honest questions:

When was the last time I enjoyed a class, regardless of the result? Do I still feel connected to my horse? Am I proud of how I handled myself, even when it did not go perfectly?

If any of the answers are a no, you are not broken. You are simply overdue for a reset.

A reset does not mean quitting. It means recalibrating. Take a pressure-free ride. Ride without a stopwatch, a goal, or an audience. Let your horse stretch. Let yourself breathe. Spend time in the saddle without asking for more than presence and feel.

Change your perspective at the show. Watch a class with no agenda other than enjoyment. Observe good riding. Appreciate horsemanship. Notice moments of partnership instead of scanning for mistakes.

Step outside the ring, literally and mentally. Walk around the barn and take in where you are. The horses, the people, the history of the sport. Remember that this life, while demanding, is also rare and earned.

Burnout is often a sign that pressure has replaced purpose. The goal is not to remove ambition, but to put it back in balance.

HOLD THE JOY

Tina Sutter, enjoying a moment with her beloved CH I'm Lookin' At You. Photo by Katherine Hansil

At its core, this sport is built on love. Love for the horses. Love for the challenge. Love for the pursuit of something difficult, humbling, and deeply personal.

Joy is not something you feel only when you win. It is something you protect. This means allowing yourself to celebrate small progress: a better connection, a calmer round, a moment where your horse tried harder because you rode better. These moments matter, even if no one hands you a ribbon for them.

It also means creating boundaries around pressure. Not every class has to be career-defining. Not every ride has to prove something. Riders who last in this sport know when to push and when to let a day be just a day.

Holding joy requires intention. Gratitude after rides, perspective after losses, presence during the process are skills, not personality traits. If you can hold onto that love, even when the stakes rise, you will ride better. You will make clearer decisions and you will stay connected to your horse and to yourself.

Ribbons fade, seasons change, careers evolve. What stays are the memories, the relationships, and the version of yourself this sport shapes. Make sure the experience you are building is one you will want to remember.

20

STUDY THE GAME

There is a difference between showing up and showing up prepared. Every rider trots through the in-gate hoping to deliver a winning performance, but the riders who consistently rise to the top did not leave their preparation to chance. They studied the game before they played it.

OBSERVE THE RING LIKE A PRO

Unless you are in the first few classes of the show, make it a priority to spend time at the ring before you show. Not to kill time or socialize, but to actively study what is happening. Watch how the judge runs their classes. Take note of how long they hold each gait, especially the walk. Pay attention to where the judge stands for the entrance, whether they move once the gate closes, which rail they focus on most, and whether they shift positions during the reverse.

Notice whether they are watching turns closely, paying attention to passes during the lineup, or using that time to organize their card. Observe whether they take their time before turning in results or move quickly to the next class. Every one of these details helps you mentally prepare for how your ride will unfold.

Do not stop with the judge. Look at the ring itself. Has anything changed since practice rides? A new flower box, uneven footing, or a banner that was not there yesterday can affect a horse's focus and a rider's composure. The energy in the stands matters too. Is the crowd loud, quiet, distracted, or reactive? Riders who pay attention enter the ring grounded while others are still reacting.

Great riders do not just watch the ring. They mentally rehearse based on what they see. As you observe, begin building a picture in your mind of where you will make your passes, where you will collect or push forward, and how you will adjust if the judge moves. By the time you enter the ring, you should already have a mental map of how you want your ride to unfold. Riders who succeed at the highest levels are not surprised by the environment. They are ready to dominate it.

THE JORDAN STANDARD: ARRIVE PREPARED, NOT HOPEFUL

Michael Jordan did not walk onto the Basketball court hoping for the best. He arrived early, not just to warm up, but to gather information. He studied the floor, tested the bounce, checked dead spots, watched how the ball came off the rim, and evaluated lighting, temperature, and spacing. He wanted every variable under control before the first whistle.

He watched opponents the same way riders should watch classes. Not to judge them, but to understand patterns, who hesitates in corners, who drifts to the rail when making passes, who tightens under pressure, who leaves an opening for a clean pass. Jordan mentally rehearsed the win long before the game started. He saw himself executing, responding, and controlling the energy before anyone else entered the arena.

That is exactly how elite riders show up. They study the ring before they ever step into it. They know the footing, the flow, the judge's habits, the timing of the class, and the strengths and weaknesses of the field. They visualize the ride they want, and by the time they trot in, they are not reacting. They are executing. Jordan did not wait to become great after the game started. He arrived great. Riders who prepare that way separate themselves every single time.

REVIEW YOUR RIDES (EVEN IF YOU HATE WATCHING YOURSELF)

I will be the first to admit I do not love watching my class videos, but I do it because video does not lie. It shows what actually happened, not what you believed was happening. When you are serious about improvement, that information is priceless.

J. B. Mauney, the legendary seven-million-dollar bull rider, has said he was not the most naturally talented. He made up for it with work ethic, preparation, grit, and brutal honesty. He watched every ride he ever made on video, analyzing the smallest details of what worked and what did not. He credited that level of review as one of the biggest reasons he became one of the greatest in his sport. He once said, *"You get on and tie your hand in there and do not quit until they stomp you loose." He did not just ride harder. He learned harder."*

When you review your videos, do not fall into emotional judging. You are not watching to beat yourself up or defend yourself. You are studying like an athlete reviewing game film: objectively, strategically, and with a mindset of growth. Ask yourself what worked, what fell apart, whether your transitions were clean, whether your passes looked as good as they felt, whether you were where you thought you were in relation to the judge, and whether your presence matched the ride you imagined.

Better yet, watch with your trainer. Someone you trust will catch details you missed. The goal is not perfection. The goal is progress.

LEARN FROM THE GREATS

One of the fastest ways to elevate your performance is to study riders who consistently execute at a high level. Sometimes that rider is a nationally recognized professional. Sometimes it is a seasoned amateur who always seems to end up near the top of the line. Titles are less important than results.

Watch how they ride the turns. Watch how they manage traffic without looking frantic. Watch how they create space, take advantage of opportunities, and protect their horse from unnecessary pressure. Pay attention to how they enter the ring and how they leave it. Strategy is happening constantly, even when it looks calm.

The best riders make it look effortless, but that ease is not accidental. It is the result of repetition, preparation, and hundreds of small, correct decisions layered together.

When you watch them, do not just admire the overall picture. Break it down. Notice their rhythm and how rarely it changes. Notice their spacing and how they never seem rushed. Notice their patience when others are panicking. Notice their timing when it matters most. Notice their composure, especially when things are not perfect. Believe it or not, those details are teachable.

Action step: At every show, pick one rider per session to study. Do not watch casually. Watch with intent. Ask yourself why they chose a certain line, why they waited instead of forcing, and how they recover when something does not go as planned. Then apply one of those observations in your own ride.

KNOW THE FIELD, RIDE YOUR RIDE

Yes, this is a competition, and yes, you should want to win. But being competitive does not mean riding against other people. It means riding with awareness.

Know who else is in your class. Understand their strengths, their habits, and the kind of rides they typically produce. Awareness helps you make smarter choices for your horse, especially in crowded or high-pressure classes.

That awareness, however, should never turn into fixation. Riders get into trouble when they start riding defensively or reactively. Watching someone else too closely leads to rushed decisions, poor spacing, and unnecessary tension. Judges see this immediately. So do horses.

The goal is informed confidence, not distraction. Ride your horse. Protect your plan. Make adjustments when necessary, but never at the expense of integrity or safety. Do not disrupt another ride. Do not manufacture chaos. Win clean. Win with class.

Action step: Before the class, identify one or two tendencies in the field that may affect traffic or spacing. Then commit mentally to riding your own rhythm regardless of what others do. If you catch yourself watching another rider too much mid-class, reset your focus to your horse's ears, your line, and your pace.

SHOWMANSHIP MATTERS

Some riders are natural "showmen," and in a judged sport, that is an advantage. But showmanship is not an exaggeration or performance for its own sake. It is presence.

Presence is controlled energy. It is knowing when to turn the switch on and when to stay quiet. It is being intentional with every movement, from how you walk into the ring to how you sit in the saddle. Judges do not respond to desperation. They respond to clarity and command.

Showmanship shows up in posture, eye line, and how you occupy space. It shows up in how you recover after a mistake without shrinking or apologizing for being there. This presence can be trained.

Action step: Practice presence outside the ring. Walk into the barn aisle like you belong there. Sit tall as soon as you mount. Take a breath before you enter the ring and commit to riding the first thirty seconds with confidence, regardless of nerves.

UNDERSTAND THE SPECS

If you truly want to understand how judges make decisions, read what most riders skip: the USEF (or other governing body) Rulebook. Each division outlines specifications in order of importance. That order matters. For example, in Saddlebred pleasure and many amateur divisions, the first word listed is manners. Not motion, not brilliance, but manners.

A brilliant horse that is resistant or reactive is not fulfilling the specifications. Judges are required to reward the horse that best meets the criteria. This is where many riders lose the plot. They chase expression without a mannerly performance. They excuse resistance because the horse is talented. They confuse energy with a quality performance. Understanding the specs removes the mystery from judging and gives you a clear framework for how to ride.

Action step: Read the specifications for your division before the season begins. Highlight the first priorities listed. Ask yourself honestly whether your ride supports those requirements. Train and show accordingly.

COMPLAINING IS NOT A STRATEGY

Every discipline has a structure, whether people like it or not. Some riders study that structure. Others fight it.

Judges consistently see riders who spend more energy explaining why they cannot succeed than figuring out how they can. They talk about what they do not have instead of working with what they do. Less money. Less time. Less access. Less support. Less opportunity. None of those realities are unique, and none of them excuse a lack of preparation.

Successful riders evaluate their current position honestly. They understand their resources, their experience, and their limitations. Then they build forward in steps that make sense. That might mean choosing the right division instead of the most impressive one. It might mean staying local longer. It might mean investing in education before upgrading horses.

Judges notice riders who are strategically climbing instead of emotionally forcing progress. Studying the game means knowing where you are, where you want to go, and what it will realistically take to get there.

ACCEPTANCE IS NOT SURRENDER

Some riders spend their entire careers angry at the system. Angry at judges. Angry at barns that win. Angry at rules they do not understand or do not want to accept. The anger feels justified to the rider. It feels like passion. But from the outside, it reads very differently.

Judges recognize this mindset quickly. It shows up in body language, post-class behavior, and how riders talk about their results. Frustration has a tone, it has posture and it has patterns. Tight hands, slumped shoulders, complaints whispered just loudly enough to be heard do not help your case.

Every sport has limits. Not every rider will play at the top level, and not every path leads to the same destination. That reality is not cruel. It is clarifying.

Acceptance is not surrender. It is actually a strategy you can use. When you accept the reality of your resources, your horse, your experience level, and the division you are in, you stop wasting energy fighting imaginary battles. You choose goals that are aligned with ability, budget, time, and personal satisfaction. From there, progress becomes measurable instead of emotional.

Riders who accept reality move forward. Riders who fight it stay stuck. Judges are not obligated to reward frustration, entitlement, or resentment. They reward performance that meets the specs, shows preparation, and reflects professionalism.

Action step: Take an honest inventory of your horse, your training, your experience, and your goals. If they do not align, adjust the goal instead of resenting the result. Acceptance clears the path for improvement.

WANT TO REALLY UNDERSTAND JUDGING? GO TO JUDGE'S SCHOOL

If you want to stop guessing why certain placings happen, there is a direct solution. Go to judge's school. You do not need to apply for a judge's card to attend. Riders, trainers, amateurs, and parents are all welcome. And it may be the most valuable education you invest in.

Judge's school teaches you what judges are trained to look for, how decisions are made, and how impressions are formed in real time. You learn how specifications are applied and why some placings make complete sense from the center of the ring, even when they look confusing from the rail. Most riders view judging as mysterious or subjective because they have never seen the process from the inside.

Once you do, everything changes. You stop taking results personally. You understand the trade-offs. You see why one mistake matters and another may not. You start riding toward the criteria instead of riding toward what you think looks impressive.

Action step: Attend a judge's school or continuing education clinic at least once. Take notes. Listen without defensiveness. Apply what you learn to your riding immediately.

WHY JUDGES JUDGE

Sandra Currier wearing the exhibitor hat instead of the clipboard.

Judging education forces you to look at a class through a completely different lens. You learn how specifications are interpreted, how priorities are weighted, and how small details separate one ride from another when everything looks "pretty good." It strips away a lot of assumptions and replaces them with clarity.

Judging has made me a better exhibitor, a better trainer, a better instructor, and a better clinician.

It sharpened my eye, raised my standards, and changed how I prepare horses and riders long before they ever trot through the gate. Standing in the center of the ring rewires how you see everything from transitions to turnout to timing.

I'm not the only one. Many professionals who have stepped into judging did not start out with that goal. They got there through experience, opportunity, and curiosity. Along the way, they discovered that judging wasn't just a credential, it was an education.

The following perspective from Sandra Currier captures that evolution perfectly and explains why understanding how judges are trained can elevate your riding, whether or not you ever plan to hold a card yourself.

I asked Sandra to explain how and why she got her judge's card. Here is what she shared with me:

"I never made a conscious decision to become a judge.

Many years ago, when I was training horses in upstate New York, I was asked to judge a few local one-day shows. I agreed because, quite honestly, the extra money helped a young trainer pay the bills.

As the years went on, I realized that if I wanted to be considered for more established, bona fide shows, I needed to attend USEF clinics and earn a real judge's card. Along the way, I also realized something else: judging is an integral part of our industry and one of the most meaningful ways to give back.

I strongly believe exhibitors should take the time to read the breed section of the rule book. It clearly outlines judging specifications and explains how manners, performance, presence, conformation, and quality are weighted differently depending on the division. Those details matter more than most people realize.

I only judge two or three shows a year, and my customers have always been supportive of the time I take away. That said, judging has made me more demanding of them as well. Standing in the center of the ring changes your perspective.

Small things often separate the top horses from the bottom ones. Upward and downward transitions, a thoughtfully planned reverse, and a crisp trot can add the extra polish that elevates a ride. My customers know to arrive with clean, polished boots and neat attire, but it wasn't until I stood in center ring that I truly understood how much those details matter.

I'll leave you with this story.

I once attended a clinic given by a very well-known pony trainer. He spoke about judging and some of the great horses and ponies he had seen, and then shared a story about the biggest argument he and his wife ever had. He had tied a class at Louisville the way he felt it should be tied. After the show, his wife told him she strongly disagreed.

That moment stuck with me. The perspective from center ring and the perspective from the seats can be very different."

IRON SHARPENS IRON

Growth does not come from comfort. Riders who improve consistently do not hide in shallow classes forever. When they are ready to, they enter deeper classes, seek stronger competition, and allow weaknesses to be exposed so they can be fixed. Pressure sharpens timing, awareness, nerves, and horses. Comfort quietly caps potential.

When you consistently ride in deeper waters, the riders who once intimidated you stop feeling untouchable. You learn their patterns. You realize they are human. You improve simply by sharing the ring with them. This is not about chasing failure. It is about choosing a challenge intentionally.

Action step: Identify one area where you have been playing it safe. A division, a level, or a class you avoid. Step into it with preparation and curiosity, not fear.

IF YOUR LAST CLASS WAS A MOVIE

Imagine your last class playing on a giant screen. The audience reacts in real time.

What would they shout?
"Don't cut that corner."
"Sit back."
"Stop rushing."
"Act like you belong."

This exercise is uncomfortable because it removes excuses. The judge sees exactly what the audience sees. Not what you intended. What actually happened.

Many people avoid watching themselves because it is hard and honestly it threatens their ego. Elite riders use video because it reveals the truth. Judges reward the ride that showed up, not the ride you hoped you delivered.

Action step:
Pick one ride. Watch it without commentary. Then watch again and write down three specific corrections. Fix those before your next class.

FINAL THOUGHT: BE THE ONE WHO PREPARES LIKE A PRO

You do not need to be wealthy, famous, or born into the sport to ride like a winner. You need to prepare like one.

Preparation is cumulative. Every class you watch with intention. Every rider you study instead of envy. Every video you review instead of avoiding, every stretch challenge you accept builds an edge most riders never develop.

Preparation compounds quietly. Eventually, it puts you exactly where you want to stand. Calm, ready and being remembered for all the right reasons. The opportunity is there. The preparation is up to you.

21

FEEL IS EARNED

"Feel can seem untouchable, like something only the chosen few are born with. But fighting to find it, ride after ride, is what turns you into a legend."

They say you can't teach feel. That it's something you're either born with or not. But let's be honest most of the time, that's just a convenient excuse.

In middle school, I got placed on the B team in basketball. I rarely played. And yes, it was embarrassing. However, I've never been someone who can stomach being mediocre at something I care about. So that summer, my dad mounted a basketball hoop inside the barn. We both knew I didn't have natural talent in the sport, but what I did have was drive. Relentless, slightly delusional, completely unshakable drive.

And if you know my dad, he's not the type to hand out praise unless it's earned. I didn't always love that, but it made me better. It made me accountable.

We practiced constantly. We played HORSE, but with one rule, your shot didn't count unless it was a swish. No backboard. No rim. Nothing but net. He raised the bar. I kept reaching.

By the time tryouts rolled around the next year, I made the A team and started as shooting guard. I wasn't headed to the WNBA, but that was never the goal. The real win came long before the first game.

Then at sixteen, a horse fell on me. My knee was injured and I needed surgery. Sadly, my basketball career ended early. Fortunately, the work ethic I learned from it stuck with me.

That was the moment I realized talent might start the race, but work ethic decides who finishes it. The same is true in riding. And if you're in a sport where feel separates the great from the average, let me say this clearly: feel is obtainable if you're willing to take full responsibility for earning it.

THE TALENT TRAP

The horse show world loves a good myth, and "natural talent" might be the most persistent one. We say things like, "She's just got a feel for it," or "He's a natural horseman," as if success is something you are born with rather than something you build. Those comments sound flattering, but they quietly imply that if it doesn't come easily, it might never come at all.

Some people do start with advantages. They may have better timing, intuition, or rhythm early on, and that head start often gets them noticed quickly. What it does not guarantee is longevity or the development of true skills. Over decades of riding, training, and judging, I have watched the same pattern repeat itself. The riders labeled as "naturals" often rely too heavily on instinct, plateau early, and stop developing. Meanwhile, the rider who studies, listens, and refuses to quit keeps improving long after the initial shine has worn off.

Talent opens doors, but work ethic determines how long you stay in the room. Judges notice talent, but they remember consistency, preparation, and improvement. When the pressure is high, the horse is difficult, or the conditions are far from ideal, talent alone is rarely enough. Preparation is what holds the ride together when instinct starts to crack.

If you are not the most naturally gifted rider in the class, that is not a disadvantage. It means you have something far more reliable available to you. Control over your preparation, your habits, and your willingness to do the unglamorous work that actually moves the needle.

WHAT FEEL ACTUALLY LOOKS LIKE

Feel is not vague, mystical, or based on intuition alone. It is specific, tactical, and earned through repetition and awareness. Feel shows up in timing, in knowing when to wait and when to ask, and in recognizing the difference between energy that is building correctly and tension that is about to derail the ride.

It is the ability to make adjustments in real time based on subtle information, such as the horse's breathing, weight shifts, or how the contact feels in your hand. It is understanding whether resistance comes from confusion, fatigue, or anxiety and responding accordingly instead of reacting emotionally.

From a judge's perspective, feel is unmistakable. It looks like a horse that stays soft through transitions and a rider whose body and hands are quiet without being passive. It looks like consistency, even when something small goes wrong. Often, the most telling sign of feel is that no one realizes the rider had to fix anything at all.

True feel is when the horse starts responding before the aid becomes obvious. That kind of responsiveness does not come from luck. It comes from trust built through repetition, patience, and presence.

COACHING FEEL

When people say a rider "just doesn't have feel," what they usually mean is that the rider has not been taught how to develop it. As I have stated before, feel is not something reserved for a select few. It is a skill, and like any skill, it requires intentional training.

One of the most effective ways to teach feel is through contrast. Riders benefit from riding the same horse multiple ways in a single session: big and forward, then soft and quiet, then more mechanical, and finally relaxed. Experiencing those differences creates clarity. Feel does not develop when everything stays comfortable and familiar. It develops when riders learn to recognize how small changes alter the horse's response.

Another critical component is removing shortcuts. Taking away stirrups, reins, or adding work on a lunge line forces riders to pay attention with their body instead of relying on habit or reaction. These tools are not punishments. They are educational. When riders lose the ability to mask mistakes, awareness increases.

Equally important is what happens the moment an instruction is given. When a rider actually implements the instruction and pays attention to how the horse and the performance change as a result, learning accelerates. The rider begins to connect cause and effect in real time. When they truly feel the difference an adjustment makes in the horse, that information sticks. The next time the same sensation shows up in a ride, the rider recognizes it and recalls the solution faster.

Teaching feel is the responsibility of the instructor, but learning feel ultimately belongs to the rider. Instruction alone is not enough. Riders must be willing to apply what they are told, notice how the horse responds, and stay present long enough for the lesson to register. That attention is what turns coaching into skill.

Feel is not instinct. It is attention applied consistently over time. Riders do not wake up with it. They earn it by listening, implementing, and observing, ride after ride. Riders who commit to that process eventually stop chasing feel, because at some point, they begin riding with it.

TALENT WITHOUT FIRE

I have a rider who has more natural talent than some professionals I know. More than some of the top riders in the industry. She has it all: feel, timing, balance, instinct. The kind of rider judges want to reward, but there's one thing missing: the fire.

She doesn't have the drive to compete. She doesn't burn to win. She doesn't care about showing the judge how great she actually is. Because of that, she gets lost in the crowd.

Yes, she gets good ribbons. Yes, she rides beautifully, but she never crosses the line into undeniable. She doesn't win in the way that makes people believe she should win. And that's the part I sometimes struggle to teach someone, but I will keep trying.

CAN YOU TEACH SOMEONE TO WANT IT?

You can drill it, ride for it, earn it. But competitive fire? I'm not so sure. I'm trying. I really am. But I've learned that desire is harder to ignite than skill is to build. If you don't want to stand out, if you're afraid to ride with presence, if your goal is to just "blend in and ride well," you'll probably never take over the class.

And if that's your goal, that's fine. But let's be honest with ourselves, if you're not here to compete, why are you competing? There's no shame in riding for fun. Trail rides, lesson barns, schooling shows with no pressure, those are all valid options. But when you choose to walk into a judged show ring, you're asking to be evaluated. So why hide?

WHY SOME RIDERS DIM THEIR FIRE

A lot of people assume this kind of rider is lazy or unmotivated, but I don't believe that. I think it is usually fear, just not fear of riding or showing. It is fear of wanting something they do not believe they can earn. Fear of the disappointment that comes from trying and falling short.

If you do not expect much from yourself, you cannot be that disappointed when it does not happen. Right? Here is the hard truth. You cannot win consistently unless you risk disappointment. You cannot be memorable unless you are willing to be seen.

What this looks like in the ring is subtle. Riders ride smaller than they need to. They pass safely instead of boldly. They avoid moments that could elevate the class because those moments also carry risk. They tell themselves they are being "realistic" or "just learning," when in reality they are managing expectations to protect their ego.

The problem is that judges can feel that restraint. Horses feel it too.

A rider who dims their fire is technically present but emotionally absent. There is no ask, no statement, no conviction. It reads as polite, careful, and forgettable. And forgettable is far more damaging than imperfect.

If this sounds familiar, the solution is not reckless riding or manufactured drama. Instead it is intentional courage. Decide before you enter the ring where you are willing to be bold. Pick one moment in the class to fully commit. One pass, one line, one transition where you stop hedging and ride like you expect it to work.

You do not need to be fearless. You just need to stop negotiating with yourself in the middle of the class.

Confidence is not pretending you cannot lose. It is accepting that you might and riding forward anyway. The riders who rise to the top are not the ones who avoid disappointment. They are the ones who decided it was not a reason to play small.

HOW I TRY TO TEACH IT ANYWAY

I have not given up on these riders, and I will not. But I also do not coddle the pattern.

I start by engineering small, undeniable wins. Not vague encouragement, but moments where they can feel the difference between riding safely and riding with intention. I do not tell them to "ride well." I tell them to own the ring from the first pass. I give them a clear objective that forces presence, not perfection.

Then I get very honest about what winning actually means. Winning is not just a ribbon. It is about strategy, and it is about commitment. It is the satisfaction that comes from knowing you did not hold anything back. Even when the result does not go your way, that feeling is unmistakable. Riders who experience it once start chasing it again.

I also make something explicit that too many riders, especially girls and young women, have never been told. You are allowed to want this and you are allowed to be intense. Wanting to win does not make you arrogant, dramatic, or unlikable. It makes you honest.

Finally, I make it safe to fail, but not comfortable to hide. Failure is part of development. Playing small is not. No rider ever rode with authority while trying to protect themselves from disappointment. Power comes from trust. Trust in the horse, the preparation, and your own ability to recover if it does not go perfectly.

My job is not to eliminate fear. It is to teach riders how to ride forward with it. Because confidence is not the absence of doubt. It is the decision to act anyway.

RIDE LIKE YOU WANT IT

Confidence and competitiveness go hand in hand. You don't need to be arrogant. You don't need to be loud. But you do need to believe you belong in the top of the class. You have to want it more than you're afraid of not getting it.

Presence, the kind that makes a judge notice you, isn't all about how you ride. It's about how you show up.

If you're still holding back, ask yourself: Do I want to be good? Or do I want to be great? Either answer is okay, but only one of them is going to get you the win.

If you've got talent, use it. If you've got fire, light it. If you've got both, stop hiding and start riding like it.

22

THE COACHABILITY FACTOR

Master the skill beneath every skill. You want to get better? Start here. Not with your horse, not with a better saddle, newer suit, or fancier bridle. You need to start with your ability to be coached.

Coachability is the foundation for all progress in this sport. It's not optional, it's critical. If you can't take direction, apply correction, and stay mentally in the game while you're on the horse, you will hit a ceiling. And it won't be your horse holding you back, it'll be you.

A lot of riders think they're coachable. They say they're open to feedback. But watch what happens when they don't get praised. Or when a trainer gives them the same correction three times in a row. Or when they lose a class they thought they had in the bag. Suddenly, they're defensive. Blaming the horse, the judge. Possibly shutting down completely.

Being coachable doesn't mean you're always smiling or nodding. It means you're able to receive direction without immediately filtering it through your ego. It means being able to hear what your trainer is saying, apply it, and ride through it without drama.

You're not just riding, you're thinking, adjusting, recalibrating, and learning on the fly. And in a judged sport, where split-second decisions make the difference between a clean ride and a missed moment, the ability to learn in real time is everything.

I used to believe I just wasn't one of those trainers/exhibitors who could win right out of the gate. I thought I needed to embarrass myself first, then reflect, then regroup. And to be honest, that's still sometimes how it happens. But here's what I've learned: even the people who do win early, still go through the same process. We all get it wrong in some capacity before we get it right. The difference is in how fast you're willing to be wrong, hear it, adjust, and try again.

Michael Jordan, who knew a few things about greatness, once said:
"My best skill was that I was coachable. I was a sponge and aggressive to learn."
That's not just humility talking, it is a mindset and it's not limited to basketball.

Former UFC champion Rashad Evans said:
"As an athlete, you have to be coachable. And being coachable is a humbling thing."
In other words: if you're too proud to be coached, you're not ready to be great.

Even in football, where talent is everywhere, legendary NFL coach Bill Belichick said:
"It's not all about talent. It's about dependability, consistency, and being able to improve. If you work hard and you're coachable, and you understand what you need to do, you can improve."

That applies to riders, too. I've worked with hundreds of riders. You know who ends up on top more often than not? The ones who can listen and don't make excuses. The ones who want to be corrected because they're obsessed with progress.

You don't need to be the most naturally gifted rider in the ring. You need to be the most coachable. The most willing to adjust. The most eager to understand what your horse needs from you and what your trainer is trying to teach you.

When you ride coachable, you're not just reacting, you're anticipating. You start to feel the rhythm of the class, the setup of the corners, the subtlety of potential cues, and most importantly, the shifts in your horse's body and mind. You learn to spot problems before they become mistakes. You begin to fine-tune the micro-adjustments that separate average rides from winning ones.

And it's not just about showing. It's about training. Horsemanship is a constant conversation, and coachability helps you become a fluent translator between your trainer's voice and your horse's feedback. The most successful people are often the most sensitive ones, not just to the horse, but to the people trying to help them ride better.

In many cases, coachability means hearing something uncomfortable and not immediately making it about your worth. It means trusting that your trainer is on your side, even when they're pushing you. It means remembering that instruction isn't an insult, it's an investment.

The trick is being coachable doesn't mean being passive. It doesn't mean waiting for every direction or losing your own instincts. Great riders merge what they know with what they're being taught. They don't just follow, they integrate. They ask smart questions. They listen more than they speak. They know when to trust their gut and when to trust the person on the rail.

Let me be blunt: If you want to make it to the top levels in this sport, and you're not willing to be coached, you're going to be lapped by people who are. Riders who are maybe a little less talented but 10 times more coachable will outpace you in every way that matters.

So how do you become more coachable? Start by staying open. Watch how you respond when someone gives you feedback, do you get defensive, or do you get curious?

And please, stop explaining every mistake and start absorbing the lesson instead.

Remind yourself: you hired your trainer or instructor for a reason. You chose this path. Let yourself be a student of the process.

This is the truth nobody wants to hear. If you can't take feedback without unraveling, if you only want praise and not direction, if your first instinct is to argue rather than learn, you're not serious about getting better. And in this sport, that will show. It will show in the ring. It will show in your horse. And it will show on the judge's card.

Ask yourself: Am I trying to look like I know what I'm doing, or am I actually trying to learn? Because only one of those leads to mastery.

REAL-TIME ADAPTABILITY

Coachability goes way beyond hearing instructions. At the top levels, riders have to absorb direction and execute it instantly while staying in rhythm with the horse and the class. That's real-time adaptability, and it's one of the clearest separators between a great rider and one who's still figuring it out.

Horses don't always feel the way you expect them to when you enter the ring. Sometimes they're hotter. Sometimes they're slow to step up. Sometimes the energy in the arena shifts the second the photographer flashes or a gate clangs. A coachable rider adjusts without falling apart. They change their cadence, their strategy, and they do it without acting like something "went wrong." They adapt like that was the plan.

Traffic in the ring is another test. Most people can ride well in an empty arena. But the riders who excel are the ones who can read a developing jam, shift lanes without drama, and adjust their path without losing presence. They stay alert, and they stay ahead of the problems instead of reacting late and blaming other horses.

And then there's the trainer's voice; the tone, not just the words. A coachable rider can decode urgency, correction, or reassurance in one second. They don't panic when the trainer's tone sharpens, and they don't collapse when the trainer demands more. They interpret it, adjust, and keep going. Real-time adaptability turns coaching into power, not pressure.

THE TRAINER'S PERSPECTIVE ON COACHABILITY

As a trainer, you know in the first five minutes who is likely going to excel. It's not always the prettiest rider. It's not the bravest rider. Though those traits can certainly help. It's the one who listens with intention and applies what you say immediately and without excuses.

The riders who rise are the ones who show up ready to work, not ready to perform for praise. They try again without being coaxed. They fix something without announcing why it went wrong. They don't rush for instant gratification; they settle into the long game. They trust that the process will get them where they want to go and that trust shows up in how they respond to correction, pressure, repetition, and challenge.

On the other hand, riders who want the shortcut, the compliment, or the quick fix plateau early. They ride for validation instead of growth. Trainers spot it instantly: the eye roll, the sigh, the "I know," the emotional wobble when the correction hits a nerve. It's not lack of talent that holds them back, it's lack of trust.

Your authority here matters. You've taught enough riders, trained enough horses, and seen enough levels of success to know exactly which behaviors predict long-term excellence. Giving readers that insider clarity helps them self-evaluate honestly.

COACHABILITY AND MENTAL TOUGHNESS

Coachability has nothing to do with compliance. It's mental toughness disguised as humility.

Emotionally fragile riders hit a ceiling fast. They crumble when corrected. They spiral when the horse feels different. They take instruction as criticism and pressure as punishment. And when things go sideways, even slightly, they abandon the plan. That fragility shows up everywhere, in warm-up, in the lineup, and especially in tight classes where mental steadiness decides the ranking.

Mentally tough riders don't unravel. They're steady. When the horse is having an off day, they don't melt down or transfer their frustration onto the rail or the trainer. They regulate themselves, adjust the plan, and ride the horse they have. That stability translates directly into calmer horses, more effective rides, and better decisions.

Mentally grounded riders also make sharper strategic choices. They don't panic when traffic shifts. They don't rush a transition out of frustration. They stay disciplined through the entire class, which makes them vastly easier to judge — and easier to reward. That's championship behavior, and it starts with coachability.

HOW COACHABILITY SHOWS UP TO A JUDGE

People seem to love to believe judges can't "see" coachability, judges usually end up seeing all of it eventually.

A coachable rider smooths out issues between passes instead of broadcasting them. They quietly make adjustments without throwing a fit in the saddle. When they make a mistake, they recover with poise instead of spiraling or over-correcting. They look like someone who can handle pressure and keep the horse steady even when things aren't perfect.

Judges also see riders who are clearly listening to their trainers, the subtle rein change, the shift in pace, the corrected corner, all done thoughtfully, not sloppily. They see riders who adjust their rail position instead of plowing into a jam. They see riders who take responsibility for their ride rather than hoping someone else moves out of their way.

Coachability reads as reliability. And reliability reads as quality. Of course, judges reward rides that show excellence but also consistency and reliability. They reward riders who handle themselves and their horses with professionalism. Those traits don't always come from talent. They come from coachability too.

RESILIENCE IS THE DIFFERENCE-MAKER

Coachability and mental toughness do not exist without resilience. Resilience is what allows a rider to absorb pressure, correction, disappointment, and uncertainty without losing their footing. It is the ability to stay engaged after something goes wrong instead of mentally checking out.

In the show ring, resilience shows up fast. A botched entrance, a crowded corner, a horse that feels different than it did at home. None of those moments are unusual. What matters is what the rider does *next*.

Non-resilient riders get stuck in the mistake. They replay it mid-class. They ride defensively afterward. They tighten, rush, or abandon the original plan entirely. From the judge's perspective, the ride starts to unravel, not because of one error, but because the rider never recovers from it.

Resilient riders reset quickly. They acknowledge the mistake internally and move on. They stay present. They keep riding forward. The class continues to build instead of deteriorate. That ability to recover is often the difference between placing in the middle and standing at the top.

Resilience also determines whether riders reach long-term goals. Every serious competitor will lose classes they thought they should win. Every rider will have a bad night under good judges. Every horse will disappoint them at some point. Riders who succeed are not the ones who avoid those moments. They are the ones who do not let those moments shrink them.

Judges reward resilience even when riders do not realize it. A rider who stays composed after trouble looks trustworthy. A horse ridden by someone mentally steady settles faster. The overall picture improves. From the card's perspective, that ride reads as mature, capable, and professional.

Resilience is not toughness for show. It is quiet durability. It is staying in the conversation when things are uncomfortable. It is riding back through the same gate tomorrow instead of sitting out because today stung.

Coachability is listening. Mental toughness is executing. Resilience is coming back ready to do it again. And in this sport, that combination wins far more often than raw talent ever will.

COACHABILITY CHANGES EVERYTHING AND THE INTERN WHO PROVES IT

I recently had a summer intern who was given more riding opportunities than most interns ever see, not just with me, but with many top trainers. People notice this and ask questions. They assume there must be a reason rooted in talent, favoritism, or relentless hustle.

The truth is much simpler, and much more important. It is not because he is wildly naturally talented. In fact, I am still not convinced that "natural" is the right word. It is not because he outworks everyone else in the barn doing chores, though he works hard. And it is not because he asks for the opportunities. He does not. He gets the rides because he is one of the most coachable riders I have worked with in years.

When he first started riding for me, my expectations were modest. He was fine. Capable. I assumed time would tell how much improvement was possible. What I did not recognize right away, and frankly recognized a little late, was what was happening every time he received actual instruction.

When given a riding correction, he applied it immediately. No commentary, no negotiation, no visible ego. He did not overthink it or try to justify what he had been doing before. He simply did what was asked, and the horse responded.

The response mattered because when the horse changed, the instruction made sense. The result was immediate feedback. He felt the difference in real time. And because he felt it, he retained it.

The next time he encountered the same situation, often on a different horse, he recalled the solution without being reminded. Not because he memorized the instruction, but because he recognized the feeling. The horse told him when it was time to apply it again. That was the moment this clicked for me.

Many riders want success just as badly. They work hard. They care deeply. They listen. But they struggle to do this one critical thing: take instruction, apply it immediately, and stay present long enough to feel what changed. Some riders hope they will remember it later. Some plan to think about it at home. Some intend to try it "next time." The time gap matters.

Everyone learns differently, but learning feel requires participation. If you want it badly enough, you can learn how to learn. You can train yourself to apply instruction on the spot, observe the horse's response, and file that sensation away for future use. That is how progress compounds.

My intern changed how I teach. I push riders harder now to implement instruction immediately. I ask them to tell me what they felt, not what they thought. I make them connect the cue to the response before the moment passes.

He also made me rethink how I learn, not just in riding, but everywhere. Just ask my Pilates instructor or, more accurately, my hamstrings, which are now very aware when I am actually doing the movement correctly. When you raise the standard for learning, it carries over into everything you do.

Coachability is not passive. It is active, disciplined, and intentional. Over time, it is one of the clearest predictors of who becomes nearly unbeatable and who, talent aside, eventually gets passed.

THE EDGE YOU CAN'T FAKE

Coachability is not a personality trait. It does give you a competitive edge. You cannot fake it, buy it, shortcut it, or talk your way into it. The naturals believe talent will bail them out, that a fancier horse or a better suit will cover the gaps. Not at the levels you are aiming for because these things don't stand the test of time and they certainly aren't the only things in play at the highest levels.

Coachability is earned in the uneventful, unglamorous moments. The corrections you absorb instead of defend. The mistakes you own instead of explaining. The lessons you apply on the very next pass instead of next week. The discipline of staying open, steady, and teachable even when your ego wants protection. That is the work that turns potential into progression and progression into performance.

Anyone can look good for thirty seconds. Coachable riders look good under pressure, under fatigue, under scrutiny, and on the days their horse feels nothing like the horse they warmed up. Coachable riders improve faster, break through ceilings sooner, and outlast the riders who depend on talent alone.

In this sport, greatness is not handed out. It is built and the riders who are willing to be coached, truly coached, are the ones who rise. Every class, every season, every year.

If you want to be unbeatable, start with being coachable. It is the foundation beneath every winning ride. It is the one skill that multiplies every other skill. And the best part is this, anyone can develop it if they are willing to leave their ego at the gate and do the work. That is the truth nobody wants to hear, but it is the truth that will change your riding forever.

23

LESSONS LEARNED

Every rider has a story they would rather forget. Usually, it is the one that taught them the most. These moments do not happen in practice rings or empty barns; they happen under the lights, in front of the people whose opinions matter most. That is where the lessons sting the hardest and stick the longest.

This is mine.

THE RIDE I LET DEFINE ME FOR TOO LONG

I had shown at the World's Championship Horse Show plenty of times before, first as a junior exhibitor and then during my short stint as an amateur during college, and with some success. I knew what it felt like to hear my name called out first in Freedom Hall. However, the first time I trotted through that gate as a professional, everything went wrong.

The horse I was showing was young and green, and so was I as a trainer. What happened next was quick and unfortunate. Another horse crashed into us, and mine reacted dramatically and noticeably. I managed to stay with him, but my ride and my pride had clearly unraveled. I remember thinking maybe, just maybe, I could quietly finish the class and no one would notice. But there is no hiding in Freedom Hall.

The crowd had seen it, or thought they had. The judges had not caught all of it, and for a moment I thought I might get lucky. Then the booing started. It rolled across the arena like a wave, and then came the shouting. I could hear a number being yelled over and over. I have always had a superstition about never looking at my back number, so I truly didn't know it was my number being shouted, and truth be told, I was praying it wasn't mine. On that day my superstition definitely was not helping my luck.

Then I saw the ringmaster heading straight for me. He pointed directly at me. The announcer made it official, I had been excused from my very first class as a professional at the most prestigious horse show in the industry. As I was making my way out of the arena, the crowd erupted again, this time in cheers. And that is how my first class as a professional in Freedom Hall ended, not just excused but literally booed out of the ring.

After that day, I never really spoke to anyone about it again. I figured if I did not say anything, maybe it would be like it never happened. And honestly, for everyone else, it probably was. Most people who were there that day have likely never thought about it again. But for me, it stuck, and for much longer than it should have.

The next year came, and I did not show on the green shavings. Then another year passed. And another. Before I knew it, eighteen years had gone by. During that time, I had brought horses and riders to Louisville. I coached them, cheered them on, and had some success. I even judged the show. But I never showed there myself. I made excuses that sounded reasonable: focused on my amateurs, did not have the right horse, too busy. I even convinced myself they were true.

The truth was simpler. I was embarrassed. And that embarrassment cost me time I cannot get back. I believe those years set me back, and I have spent every one since trying to make up for it.

For years I thought telling that story would make people think less of me, that it would confirm what I feared most, that maybe I was not good enough. What I did not realize was that by sharing it, I could help someone else avoid the same mistake. Until a few years ago, not one of my current riders even knew it happened. Then one of them had a very rough ride at Louisville and wasn't able to finish her class. She wanted to quit, to take a break, to hide like I once did. That was the moment I finally told her.

Saying it out loud changed everything. I did not expect it to, but it did. The weight I had carried for eighteen years lifted in a way I cannot explain. By helping her, I finally helped myself.

And she did not quit. I would not let her. She stayed in the game, kept showing, and she is a stronger rider and horsewoman because of it.

That is the lesson. If you fall short in front of a crowd, do not disappear. Do not wait until it feels safe again. There is no such thing as the right time to come back, there is only next time. Hiding does not protect you, it just prolongs the pain. The boos fade, the crowd forgets, but the regret of sitting out lasts for as long you let it.

So, if you have had a bad ride, an embarrassing moment, or a class that shook your confidence, get back in the ring. Do not wait eighteen years to prove to yourself that one bad day does not define your entire story. The only way forward is through the same gate you fell apart in.

What I have learned from this is that you cannot outlast fear of embarrassment. You have to outwork it. You have to outshow it. And the only thing worse than being booed out of the ring is never riding back in to change the ending.

THE MORNING AFTER THE BIG WIN OR THE BIG DISAPPOINTMENT

The interesting thing about winning at the most prestigious horse show in the Saddlebred industry is this: outside of our world, no one cares.

And here is the flip side that no one talks about. Outside of our world, no one cares if you blew it. No one cares if you got excused. No one cares if you missed a transition, had a rough class, or fell off. And that is actually comforting.

On Saturday night, you may feel like a hero. The ribbon is fresh, the roses are perfect, and your name has been announced under the spotlight. By Sunday morning, you are standing in line at a Pilot Truck Stop with long-haul drivers, waiting for coffee that tastes like regret, and no one has any idea who you are or what kind of week you just had.

I am a very hands-on horse trainer, sometimes to a fault. Some would call me a control freak. Others would say I simply trust my standards more than delegation. Either way, my dad and I still haul horses across the country ourselves several times a year, with help of course. So when I say that absolutely no one at the Pilot Truck Stop cares who you are or what you won, I mean that literally.

Within our industry, trainers who achieve consistent success, especially at the World Championship level, can feel like celebrities. There is recognition, admiration, and sometimes an inflated sense of importance that comes with it. But the moment you pull out of the Kentucky State Fairgrounds, all of that disappears.

The ribbons mean nothing. The roses mean nothing. The titles mean nothing.

And that anonymity cuts both ways. It allows you to recover quietly after a tough week. It gives you space to process disappointment without an audience. You can replay a class, feel what you need to feel, regroup, and reset without explaining yourself to anyone. There is no commentary. No judgment. No pressure to perform resilience on demand. Take advantage of that.

The riders and trainers who last in this industry understand this balance. They enjoy the wins without clinging to them, and they absorb the losses without letting them define them. They know the real test is not how they behave when they are celebrated, but how they carry themselves when no one is watching.

Because eventually, everyone ends up in the same place. Tired. Grimy. Standing in line for coffee. Just another person hauling horses down the road.

And I think that is a good thing.

5 THINGS I'D TELL MY YOUNGER SELF ABOUT COMPETING AT THE HIGHEST LEVEL

When I was twelve, Louisville looked magical and effortless. The green shavings, the roses, the spotlight; it seemed like all you had to do was ride well and the rest would fall into place.

I was wrong. And while I use Louisville as the example, these truths apply to any major horse show, any high level of competition, anywhere.

1. The competition is always deeper than you think.

- No matter how ready you feel, there is always another rider, another horse, another barn that has been grinding just as hard. At the top level, talent is assumed. Practically everyone can ride and they can present. The real difference comes from the details: preparation, strategy, mental toughness, and how well you perform under pressure.

- **Riders:** Respect the level you are stepping into. Bring your sharpest focus and your best ride every time, because someone else certainly will. At this level, hesitation is the same as handing the class away.
- **Trainers:** Do not assume past results guarantee future wins. Each season the standard rises. The riders who win consistently are the ones who innovate and adapt.
- **Owners and Parents:** Recognize that this depth is part of the journey. It may take years of persistence before your team breaks through consistently at the highest levels. Patience is not passive. It is a form of investment.

2. It costs more than you think.

- At some point you will sit down with a client, or with your own checkbook, and realize that one class required a small fortune. Travel, tack, horse care, entries, training, clothing, stabling, none of it is cheap. That is when you understand that passion does not always pencil out. But passion is what keeps us all in the game.
- **Riders:** Understand the investment behind you. Every entry fee, shoeing bill, and training ride deserves your commitment and focus. When you step in the ring, you are riding on the shoulders of sacrifice, both yours and someone else's.

- **Trainers:** Be honest with your owners about costs. Surprises are worse than reality. A well-prepared owner is a long-term owner.
- **Owners and Parents:** Remember that you are investing in growth, development, and experiences, not just ribbons. The real return is in resilience, confidence, and the discipline your rider will carry into every part of life.

3. Excitement and disappointment are neighbors.

- One moment you are floating, the next you are gutted. Sometimes both happen in the same class. You can lay down the best ride of your life and still not win, or you can have an average class and get called higher than you expected. That emotional whiplash is not a flaw of the sport. It is part of what makes it unforgettable.
- **Riders:** Do not let one class define your identity. The highs and lows are both temporary. What lasts is how you carry yourself through them.
- **Trainers:** Set the example of resilience. If you model composure, your riders will follow. They will learn that disappointment is information, not failure.
- **Owners and Parents:** Be a steady presence. Riders and trainers will remember who supported them when things went wrong far more than who cheered when things went right.

4. By the end, you will be exhausted.

- Your feet will hurt, your voice will crack, and your body will feel ten years older. You will be sore from riding, stiff from standing, and mentally fried from hours of decision-making. But exhaustion is proof that you left everything in the arena, the warm-up, and the barns.

- **Riders:** Take care of yourself. Sleep, nutrition, and hydration are not luxuries. They are part of being an athlete. Champions train their bodies to outlast pressure.
- **Trainers:** Plan your workload so exhaustion does not spill over into poor decision-making. Systems and preparation matter more here than at any other show. A tired trainer makes mistakes that ripple through an entire team.
- **Owners and Parents:** Recognize that fatigue will make tempers shorter. Patience and perspective go a long way during long weeks. Sometimes the best support is simply giving someone space to recover.

5. And yet, you will already be planning next year.

- Before the last horse is loaded, your mind will already be running strategy. Big shows are addictive. They test you, they bruise you, and they inspire you to come back sharper. The best competitors never leave thinking, "That's it, I'm done." They leave thinking, "Next year, we will fix this. Next year, we will be stronger."
- **Riders:** Ask yourself what you will do differently to raise your game. The work starts now. Greatness is built in the off-season.
- **Trainers:** Treat every class as data. What needs tightening? Which horses are ready for more? Which riders need another year to develop? Champions analyze, adjust, and attack the next season with fresh perspective.

- **Owners and Parents:** Encourage patience. Success at the highest levels is rarely immediate. It builds layer by layer. Remind your rider that what feels like failure today may be the foundation of next year's breakthrough.

Progress in this sport rarely looks like a straight line. It looks like recalibration. Riders often resist change because change feels like failure. Moving divisions feels like giving up. Selling a horse feels like admitting defeat. Slowing down feels like falling behind. Judges see it differently.

Some of the most successful careers are built by riders who know when to pivot. They step sideways to move forward. They change goals before frustration hardens into resentment. They make adjustments early, before poor habits and bitterness take hold.

Learning does not disappear just because direction changes. Experience carries forward. Confidence carries forward. Judges respect riders who make thoughtful adjustments instead of stubbornly repeating the same mistakes.

If something is not working, changing course is not a weakness. It is competence.

FINAL REFLECTION

This is what the top level really is, brutal, magical, unforgettable. It will test every part of you, your skill, your finances, your resilience, and your patience. At the same time, it will also reward you with lessons and memories no small ring can provide.

If I could tell my twelve-year-old self one last thing, it would be this: *The show is never just about the ribbon. It is about who you become in the process of chasing it.*

24

CONSISTENCY COUNTS MORE THAN THE HIGHLIGHT REEL

"But did you see that pass?"
Yes. I saw that pass. And the seven before it. And the two after.

Judges do not evaluate a ride on one shining moment. We evaluate the entire class: both directions of the ring, all required gaits, every transition, and every pass in front of us. A class is not a highlight reel. It is a body of work.

THE PROBLEM WITH RIDING FOR HIGHLIGHTS

Many exhibitors believe that if they can deliver one or two spectacular passes, the judge will overlook or forget the rest. A brilliant moment helps, but that is not how classes are decided.

A strong pass loses its impact when it is surrounded by flat, messy, or inconsistent riding. The opposite is also true. One average pass does not ruin an otherwise solid performance. Judges are far more forgiving of a small dip in quality than they are of a ride that spikes and collapses.

Consistency tells us who you really are as a rider. Highlights only show what you can do when everything lines up perfectly.

THE SILENT CONSISTENCY KILLERS

Inconsistency is not necessarily dramatic. It is subtle, which is exactly why riders sometimes miss it.

It shows up when corners are wasted instead of used to prepare for the next pass. In transitions that are rushed because the rider is already thinking about what comes next. In a horse that gets tighter with each round instead of more settled and comfortable. None of these moments feel catastrophic, but they add up quickly.

Judges notice when quality drops from pass to pass. We notice when a rider prepares beautifully for one moment and then mentally checks out afterward. Consistency is not just about brilliance. It is about sustaining focus when nothing exciting is happening.

Many riders lose consistency because they ride in bursts instead of maintaining a steady baseline. They spike their effort for a highlight, then coast. That pattern reads clearly from the middle.

YOUR BASELINE MATTERS MORE THAN YOUR BEST MOMENT

Every ride has a baseline. That baseline is what the judge sees most of the time. If your baseline is sharp, correct, and purposeful, a strong pass elevates the entire ride. If your baseline is sloppy, hurried, or unfocused, even a great pass struggles to overcome it.

Judges place the ride that stays solid over the ride that spikes and collapses. Not because we dislike brilliance, but because brilliance without structure is unreliable.

Ask yourself this question honestly: If your best pass disappeared from the class, would the rest of your ride still be competitive? If the answer is no, consistency is your work.

CONSISTENCY BEATS A MOMENT OF BRILLIANCE

I once judged a highly competitive Open Five-Gaited class that came down to two top horses. On any given night, either one could have won. The quality was there on both sides. That night, however, the difference was consistency. One horse showed up correct, bright, and engaged at every gait, every round, both directions of the ring. The quality stayed present instead of spiking and disappearing. The other horse was nice, but largely flat through most of the class. During the second way rack, he delivered two truly brilliant passes. They were exciting and unmistakable. But after each of those moments, the quality dropped right back to where it had been for the rest of the class. From the middle, that inconsistency matters. Those two brilliant passes did not outweigh the rest of the performance. They did not erase the lack of presence before and after them. They did not change the fact that the other horse delivered quality consistently, without interruption, for the entire class. So the winner was not the horse with the highest peak. The winner was the horse with the strongest body of work. This is where riders often misread results. One or even two brilliant moments do not trump a performance that shows up correct, bright, and prepared every round. Judges reward what holds together, not what flashes and fades.

WHY THIS STORY MATTERS

This example reinforces an important truth that judges are not scoring isolated moments. We are evaluating an entire body of work. Brilliance that appears briefly and disappears creates uncertainty. Consistency builds confidence. And in a judged sport, confidence in what we are seeing is what allows us to reward it.

When two horses are close, consistency becomes the separator. Not excitement. Not potential. Not what *could* have been if all the stars aligned, but what actually happened, from start to finish.

Consistency builds trust. When you deliver the same quality at every gait and on every pass, the judge knows what to expect. That reliability earns respect and higher placings. It shows that both you and your horse are trained, disciplined, and in control.

For riders, your job is not to prove you can look great once. It is to ride in a way that proves you can deliver again and again. The focus should be on the entire ride, not just a moment.

THE JUDGE'S PERSPECTIVE

When a judge sees inconsistency, it creates doubt. Was that brilliant pass the real deal or a fluke? Was that weak moment rider error, horse tension, or lack of preparation? Doubt is dangerous in a judged sport. When a performance is consistent, the judge sees confidence, presence, and reliability. That clarity makes the ride easier to reward.

THE CALL TO ACTION

Stop riding for the single highlight. Start riding for the entire class. Every stride, every corner, and every transition is part of the conversation you are having with the judge. A class is not a series of isolated moments, it is one continuous performance. Build your passes into a story that makes sense from beginning to end. Let quality stack quietly with smooth transitions, steady cadence, thoughtful positioning, presence that never drops, even in moments that feel less exciting.

Every second in front of the judge is providing information. Decide what story you want to tell, then ride in a way that supports it without interruption.

25

JUDGES IN THE WILD (AND OTHER MOMENTS YOU'RE STILL BEING JUDGED)

How you carry yourself outside the ring shows up when you ride into it.

Let's set the scene: You're at the hotel breakfast buffet, still half-asleep, balancing a sad banana and an even sadder waffle on a flimsy paper plate and you lock eyes with *the judge*. Yes, *that* judge. The one who holds your fate, or at least your class placing, in their clipboard. Cue the awkward silence. Do you say something? Smile? Pretend to study the yogurt selection like it's a legal document?

FIRST THINGS FIRST: DON'T PANIC

Let's start by acknowledging that judges are actual people. They're not magical ribbon fairies or mythical creatures who disappear into a cloud of glitter between classes. They stay at the same hotels. They wait in the same elevator lines. Sometimes, they even like pancakes.

And while your polite "hello" at the coffee station should *never* influence your placing in the ring, your behavior in these

SOCIAL MEDIA, TAGGING, AND DIGITAL OVERSHARING

Let's take it online for a minute. Social media is a powerful tool but it's also a public stage. Think before you post. Especially if the judge is tagged, present, or could be watching. That snarky caption? The vague complaint post? The sarcastic story with a "just kidding" at the end? It sticks.

Judges aren't combing your feed for reasons to pin you lower, but don't underestimate the impact of your digital behavior on your reputation. *Screenshots are forever, and the horse world is small.*

Post like a professional. Be classy, even in disappointment. Save the venting for your private circle. The confidence it takes to handle tough outcomes with grace online is the same kind of confidence that builds champions in the ring.

PARKING LOTS, WARM-UP RINGS, AND BARN AISLES

You're still being watched even when you're not "on."

Consider how you treat your horse, your trainer, your groom, etc. in the warm-up ring. How you speak to your family, your trainer, or your groom in the barn aisle. How you react to stress in the parking lot. These moments sometimes reveal more than your show ring performance.

No one is looking for perfection, but consistency in your character is powerful. I truly believe, eventually, your energy outside the ring becomes your energy inside it.

Carry yourself with presence everywhere, and your presence in the ring will carry you further than any ribbon ever could.

CONFIDENCE, CLASS, AND HUMAN NATURE

You can't control who's around you, where you might cross paths with a judge, or how your class is pinned, but you *can* control how you show up in every moment. Be the kind of rider who's consistent, composed, and kind in the ring, in the hallway, in the stall aisle, and in the comments section.

Not because it will get you a better ribbon because it won't. Do it because being that kind of person makes you a better competitor, a stronger athlete, and someone who naturally commands respect. These traits show up when you trot through the gate.

COACH'S CORNER: YOU'RE ALWAYS SETTING THE TONE

Great riders don't just ride well, they carry themselves well. Your show ring strategy doesn't begin at the in-gate. It starts at the hotel, the warm-up ring, the breakfast line. Judges notice the small things, such as your demeanor, your sportsmanship, your presence. Not to change your ribbon, but to form a fuller picture of who you are as a competitor.

So the next time you see the judge in the wild, remember this: Be calm. Be kind. Be coachable.

In this sport, someone's always watching and you want to be known for more than your ribbon count. You want to be known for your *character*.

SOMEONE IS ALWAYS WATCHING

At any given show, it's not just the official center-ring judges observing the action. Many of the trainers, instructors, and coaches working the rail are also licensed judges, or seasoned

26

CONTACTING JUDGES AFTER THE SHOW. WHEN (AND HOW) TO ASK FOR FEEDBACK

Once the show is officially over and the judge is off the clock, you're free to approach, but keep a few things in mind. First, remember that judges are human. They're tired, probably hungry, and they're ready to head home just like you. Timing is everything. Don't ambush them in the parking lot or while they're eating dinner. A little respect goes a long way.

If you do get a chance to ask for feedback, be concise and open-minded. Ask for an honest assessment.

At some point, almost every serious rider or trainer wants to know:
"What did the judge think of me?"
"Why didn't we place higher?"
"What can I do to improve?"

It's a fair instinct, however how and why you approach a judge after a show matters just as much as the questions you ask. If you're mad about your placings and know you won't be able to take constructive criticism with a level head, don't contact the judge. At best, it won't help you. At worst, it could give you a reputation as a bad sport and trust me, that reputation will follow you longer than a single disappointing ribbon. If you genuinely want feedback in order to improve your performance and get better results in the future, then reaching out can be a smart move. Most judges are happy to give honest, constructive feedback when approached politely and with genuine interest.

That said, a few tips from real-world experience:

Unless you're absolutely sure your text message will come across the right way, call instead. Tone is hard to convey over text, and I've seen good intentions turn into bad feelings simply because the message didn't land the right way. Don't assume the judge remembers your horse or rider immediately. Some shows are long. Some classes are huge. We're human. We might not remember the sixth-place horse in class 128 after judging 234 classes that week.

If possible, send a picture of your horse along with your inquiry. It helps jog our memory and makes it much easier to give specific feedback. Be polite and realistic. If the judge doesn't remember, don't get upset. If they do remember, thank them for taking the time to share their thoughts, even if the feedback is tough to hear.

LET ME GIVE YOU TWO REAL EXAMPLES:

The Wrong Way

- A trainer once contacted me after a large show, upset that I couldn't immediately remember their rider, who actually received no ribbon in a 15-horse pleasure qualifier. They approached it with a "why didn't you place us higher" tone. They couldn't believe I didn't remember them, and truthfully, to this day, I still feel annoyed about that conversation. It was a lose-lose situation for both of us.

The Right Way

- Another trainer, who had a strong show overall, reached out to ask about a specific horse's placing and they asked it completely differently. Instead of assuming I should remember, they acknowledged that I might not, sent a picture as a courtesy, and phrased it as, "If there is anything we can do to place higher, I would appreciate your feedback." Same question as the first trainer, but delivered with genuine curiosity instead of accusation. They thanked me for my time and said they valued my opinion. I left that conversation with even more respect for that trainer than I had before and I still remember the interaction fondly today.
- The impression each one left on me was night and day. You will always put yourself in a far better position with a judge (or anyone in your life) when your approach shows respect instead of entitlement or blame.

The choice is yours: You decide which way you want a judge to feel about you after the show is over.

APPROACHING FOR FEEDBACK (AND WHAT NOT TO DO)

Let's get this out of the way early: complaining to a judge about your placing is never a good look. No matter how strongly you feel, or how many people tell you that you were robbed, hunting down a judge to gripe or demand answers is the fastest way to make sure you're remembered for all the wrong reasons.

If you want to talk to a judge during or after a show, there's only one reason that makes sense: to ask for feedback. And even then, you'd better approach it with respect, patience, and a willingness to listen. Feedback is not the same as validation. You may hear things you don't like, and that's the point, if you already had all the answers, you wouldn't be asking.

THE OFFICIAL WAY: USEF RULES ON APPROACHING JUDGES

There are actual rules around this, especially at USEF-licensed competitions. **According to section GR1304.8 of the USEF rulebook:**

> *"No one shall approach a judge with regard to a decision unless he first obtains permission from the Show Committee, steward, or technical delegate who shall arrange an appointment with the judge at a proper time and place. No exhibitor has the right to inspect the judge's cards without the judge's permission."*

In plain English: You can't just walk up to the judge at the out-gate and start a conversation about your ride. You must go through the proper channels. If you want feedback during a show, you need to contact the Show Committee or the steward and have them set it up at the judge's convenience, not yours.

For non-rated shows, these steps aren't required, but that doesn't mean you should toss manners out the window. It's still in good taste to check with show management before tracking down a judge for a post-class chat.

A PATH TOWARD TRANSPARENCY AND BETTER POST SHOW CONVERSATIONS

Something I wish existed in this sport, and something I am seriously considering implementing myself, is a consistent post show platform where judges can explain their decisions. Not to defend themselves. Not to argue. Simply to clarify. The truth is that sometimes the placings are obvious to us in center ring and completely unclear to the exhibitors, trainers, and spectators watching from the rail. There are moments when what appears confusing from the outside has a very straightforward explanation that we cannot give without risking protocol violations or the appearance of being defensive.

I want people to understand why I make the choices I make. I want them to know what I valued, what separated one horse from another, and what the deciding factors were. When those explanations are missing, people are left guessing. That guessing creates tension, frustration, and mistrust. Transparency encourages growth. It keeps people participating. It strengthens the sport.

One example still stands out to me and it is the perfect illustration of how this could work. A few years ago, I judged a competitive show on a three judge panel. Several barns had very good shows and earned their placings. A couple of days later, one of those trainers called me. He thanked me for judging, then asked where he and his riders could improve. At first I was confused because he and his team had been tied consistently at the top of my card. I even said, didn't I tie you well the whole show. He said yes and that he respected my opinion, which was exactly why he was reaching out. He said, I know we won a lot, but there is always something we can do better and that becomes even more important as we head into bigger shows. The way he approached it was humble, thoughtful, and strategic. I was impressed and I found myself thinking, why am I not doing this after my own shows.

And here is what is worth pointing out. That trainer has continued to be tied at or near the top in every major horse show they attend. Obviously they are good at their job. But I do not think it is a coincidence that their willingness to seek constructive criticism and actually implement feedback is part of what keeps them successful. Their approach creates a competitive advantage, not because they are asking for favors, but because they are refusing to coast on a good performance. They want to improve, even when they are already winning.

The honest answer to why I have not adopted this approach myself is not that I fear feedback. It is that I have worried another judge might misunderstand the intention and take offense. And that should not be the case. Most judges would welcome a sincere, respectful conversation about improvement. What stops riders and trainers from asking is the old myth that questioning a judge is rude, disrespectful, or could somehow hurt them in the future. That thinking is outdated. Judges want exhibitors to understand why we made the decisions we made. We want people to show at the top of their game. We want a stronger, more informed industry.

The bottom line is: We need a better structure for transparency in our post show processes. We need to make judges more accessible for genuine feedback. We need riders and trainers to feel comfortable seeking clarity without feeling like they will be labeled a bad sport or make a judge defensive. If the goal is improvement, honesty, and long-term participation, then building a culture where open communication is encouraged is not optional. It is necessary for the future of the sport.

27

IT'S JUST A HORSE SHOW. WHEN DISAGREEING WITH THE JUDGE GOES TOO FAR

Let's get one thing clear. I do not take this sport lightly. This is my career, my passion, and the thing I have dedicated my entire adult life to. I have built a business, trained world caliber horses, taught riders at all levels, and judged at some of the biggest and most prestigious horse shows in the world. I have missed holidays, skipped vacations, and sacrificed more time, money, and energy than most people will in a lifetime. Therefore, when I say I take this seriously, I mean it.

With this in mind, it is important to remember, perspective still matters. We are showing horses, not managing an international crisis, and somewhere along the way that distinction has started to blur for some people. This is a competition. Everyone wants to win. Everyone wants their work validated, their horse appreciated, and their number called. Everyone standing at that in-gate has spent a small fortune to be there. All of that is real and valid.

What is not acceptable is allowing a judge's decision to ruin an entire day and beyond or justify harassing another human being. When that happens, the point of the sport has been lost. This chapter is not about minimizing passion. It is about managing reactions. In judged sports, exhibitors are paying for one thing: an informed opinion. That is the agreement made the moment an entry is submitted.

Judges are expected to work with focus, integrity, and competence. No one disputes that. Perfect decisions, however, do not exist. What does exist is a clear line between disagreeing with a call and crossing it as a human being.

Anyone who has spent enough time at horse shows has seen emotional reactions. A disappointed look, a frustrated sigh, or a tense walk back to the barn are normal responses to competition. Emotion is part of the process. The problem is that it does not always stop there anymore. Though it doesn't happen often, judges have been publicly yelled at, harassed online, followed, and threatened over a single class result. In some cases, the most aggressive reactions do not even come from the trainers, riders or owners directly involved. They come from spectators, fans, or individuals who were never responsible for the horse, the rider, or the decision made in the ring.

THE CROWD'S STORY MEETS REALITY

One of the most controversial World's Grand Championship classes in recent memory made this painfully clear. Fortunately, two of the judges of that class agreed to share their stories with us. Clark Clouse and Heather Boodey were members of the same three-judge panel and officiated the same class. Though, they judged from different sides of the ring, with different views of the class. Contrary to some popular conspiracy theories, they have both stated they did not discuss favorites, predictions, or anticipated outcomes before the class. In the end, their judges' cards were identical from top to bottom.

The above facts alone should have ended the conversation. Unfortunately, it did not.

The crowd had a clear favorite going in and they remained loyal throughout the class, and the energy in the building made it obvious who the audience wanted on top. When that horse was not called out as the World Grand Champion, and when the class winner did not match the expected storyline, the reaction escalated quickly. However, neither Clark nor Heather anticipated what was coming.

Heather did not initially realize there was a problem. She judged the class according to the specifications, turned in her card, and moved on. It was not until later, and then fully the next day, that she understood the magnitude of the outrage. Thankfully, the backlash was not widespread, but it was intense. Two individuals crossed the line publicly and aggressively, and the behavior was severe enough that Heather felt somewhat threatened walking out of the ring. At first, she assumed it was random noise from the crowd. It became clear very quickly that it was targeted and this behavior is unacceptable.

Clark experienced the same aftermath from a slightly different perspective. The trainers directly involved ultimately handled the situation professionally. The outrage came largely from people who were not actually involved with the specific horses, the training, or the decisions made in the ring. Much like professional sports team fans fighting or acting out after a major loss.

Heather received dozens of calls in the forty-eight hours that followed from respected trainers and close friends, all telling her the same thing: they respected and understood her decisions. One trainer involved was upset initially and then asked her why she tied the class the way she did. Once Heather explained her reasoning, the situation de-escalated. The contrast was clear. Professionals asked questions. Outsiders made a scene. This situation also illustrates how important it is that we prioritize transparency in judging.

The steward offered Heather the option to file a complaint with USEF. She declined, hoping the individuals involved would recognize how far they had crossed the line and reflect on their behavior. That decision reflected restraint, not weakness.

When asked why that particular class caused such extreme reactions, Heather pointed to something every experienced competitor understands. High stakes championship classes amplify emotion. Everyone believes they have worked harder than anyone else. Expectations are built sky-high by trainers, owners, and entire teams long before the class ever enters the ring. When reality does not match the story that has been told, disappointment can turn into frustration, and frustration can turn into anger very quickly.

Some relationships changed after that class, and some grudges remained. Heather admitted she briefly considered never judging again. The thought lasted only seconds. Out of more than one hundred classes she judged, only one created backlash. She loves judging and believes it is something horsemen should do, not only to give back to the industry, but to become better trainers and instructors themselves.

Her advice to other judges is direct. Walk away. You cannot argue with an angry person. Hold your head up and stand by your card. She welcomes conversations after the show, once emotions have settled, and encourages exhibitors to watch their videos, review the entire class, and reflect before calling a judge. In her experience, clarity often comes once the adrenaline fades. The situation did not harm her business, but it clarified who her real friends were. It also reinforced something she now emphasizes to her clients regularly: the view from center ring is different.

This situation matters because it highlights an uncomfortable truth. Two judges, judging independently from different vantage points, turned in identical cards. That reality makes it clear that backlash is not always about fairness. Judges can follow the rulebook precisely, agree completely, and still become targets for behavior that has no place in the sport.

JUDGING ISN'T EASY EVEN WHEN YOU'RE GOOD AT IT

Judging is not easy, even for people who are good at it and enjoy it. Anyone who has never judged tends to believe they would get it right every time. Judging from center ring is a completely different experience. Judges track multiple horses simultaneously, read each pass while managing spacing and traffic, and make decisions without a pause button, a replay, or reassurance in real time. Decisions are made under pressure, knowing someone will be unhappy regardless of the outcome. Most judges are doing the best they can with what they see at that moment. They are not judging reputations. They are judging performances and quite frankly, there is not enough time to do anything else.

Disappointment is allowed. Questions are allowed. Thinking a ride deserved more is allowed. I've had plenty of those moments myself. Attacking someone's character over a ribbon is not. Every time someone lashes out at a judge, spreads gossip about a class being rigged, or posts thinly veiled accusations online, the standard of the entire sport drops. This industry does not need more anger in the barn aisle. It needs more professionalism, more composure, and more people who understand that being a horseman means showing grace, especially when the result is not what they hoped for.

At the end of the day, we are showing horses. These animals do not know what class it is. They do not care what color ribbon they receive. They are not here to validate egos. If love for the sport disappears the moment winning does, it is worth asking why someone is really here. This sport will humble people. It will test patience, confidence, finances, and the ability to stay composed when things do not go their way. And still, people come back, because they love it.

The competitors who earn the most respect are the ones who lose with dignity. They thank the judge, pat their horse, and walk out already thinking about how to improve. That is sportsmanship. That is legacy. Take the sport seriously. Work hard. Aim high. Keep perspective. It is a horse show, not a character test, unless someone chooses to make it one

THE SPORT DOESN'T OWE YOU A RIBBON

Let's remind ourselves what we're really doing here. We're showing horses. These animals don't know what class it is. They don't care what color ribbon they get. They're not here to feed your ego. They're here because you brought them and because at some point, this was supposed to be fun.

If your love for the sport disappears the moment you don't win, maybe it's time to ask yourself why you're really here. Because this sport will break your heart sometimes. It will humble you. It will test your confidence, your patience, your checkbook, and your ability to stay focused when things don't go your way.

And still, you come back. Because you love it. Because you believe in your horse. Because somewhere deep down, you know it's worth it.

WIN WITH GRACE. LOSE WITH MORE.

The riders and trainers I respect most are the ones who can lose with dignity. Who thank the judge anyway. Who walk out of the ring already thinking about how to improve. Who smile, pat their horse, and move on. That's real sportsmanship. That's the kind of competitor people root for, long after the class is over.

We're in this for the long game. You won't always agree with the outcome, and that's okay. But how you handle those moments? That's your legacy. So yes, take it seriously. Work hard. Aim high. But don't forget why you started. Love the horse more than the ribbon. Respect the game more than your own pride. And when things don't go your way? Just remember: It's a horse show. Not a character test. Unless you make it one.

28

RAIL DISTRACTIONS, COACHING, CHEERING, AND CROSSING THE LINE

A crowd gathered on the rail in Freedom Hall

Let me start with a confession. I can be one of those trainers on the rail. You know the type, animated, loud, maybe a little too emotionally invested in every step my rider takes. And I know it's annoying because I'm annoyed by people like me.

Not long ago, after posting a reminder about respectful rail behavior on social media, I found myself on the receiving end of a real-time callout at a horse show. A spectator turned to me mid-class and said, "I think you're annoying the judge." She wasn't wrong. I laughed, took the hit, and (mostly) toned it down for the rest of the show. It was the perfect reminder: none of us are immune to getting swept up in the moment.

It is safe to say that how we behave on the rail matters almost as much as how our riders behave in the ring. As a judge, I can tell you with full certainty, there's a fine line between supporting your rider and becoming an unintentional distraction. Cross that line, and you're not just annoying the judge, you might be sabotaging the very ride you're trying to help.

This chapter is aimed directly at coaches, instructors, and trainers who care about developing not just great riders, but a stronger, more respected sport overall.

WHY RAIL BEHAVIOR MATTERS

From a judge's perspective, excessive noise and arm waving on the rail are distracting, sometimes even disrespectful. It can pull focus away from the riders in the ring and lower the overall professionalism of the class. Worse yet, it can negatively impact the perception of your rider, your barn, and your personal reputation.

When we behave like classy professionals, we elevate the presentation of the whole team. When we behave like unhinged sports parents, we hurt everyone.

THE FINE LINE: SUPPORT VS. DISTRACTION

There's nothing wrong with enthusiasm, encouragement, or even the occasional well-timed coaching cue. But there's a clear difference between inspiring your rider…and stealing the show.

Here's a simple litmus test:
If someone filmed the class, would you be the most memorable part of it, for all the wrong reasons?
Your job is to set your rider up for success, not to become the main character on the rail.

Supportive behavior:

- Quiet coaching when necessary
- Encouraging gestures or words without disrupting the class
- A composed, confident presence

Distracting behavior:

- Shouting nonstop across the ring
- Running up and down the rail with frantic energy
- Throwing your arms around like you're directing traffic at a busy intersection

WE HAVE TO POLICE OURSELVES

It's on us to set the standard.

If we don't hold ourselves and each other accountable, we risk turning our sport into a circus. To the general public, or even to new horse show parents and first-time spectators, our behavior can look absolutely ridiculous. Imagine a horse show dad attending his first event, watching a sea of adults shrieking, arm-waving, and sprinting along the rail. Not exactly the image of sophistication and sportsmanship we want to project.

The truth is, no one will want to join our sport if we keep acting like lunatics on the rail. We want to inspire. We want to motivate. We want to lead. We don't want to look unprofessional, unhinged, or unsportsmanlike.

Remember: every time we stand on the rail, we're ambassadors for the next generation of riders and for the health of the sport itself.

THE COST OF DISORDER

When rail behavior crosses the line, the consequences are real:

- Riders lose focus and ride defensively rather than proactively.
- Judges get distracted and irritated (never a good thing).
- Our barns earn reputations and not the good kind.
- New families and outside spectators are turned off.

Even if you "win" that day, it's a hollow victory if you win by contributing to the chaotic behavior instead of showing leadership.

REPUTATION IS HARD TO REBUILD

One bad show where your barn is known as "that group" on the rail can undo years of hard work. Judges remember. Fellow trainers remember. Parents sitting in the stands remember.

Reputation travels faster than ribbons and it's a lot harder to fix. It is a lot easier to build a culture of professionalism now than it is to dig yourself out of a hole later.

HOW TO SHOW UP ON THE RAIL

Want to help your rider, and your entire team, shine? Here's how to hold yourself to a higher standard:

- **Use calm, clear coaching.** Save the shouting for emergencies only.
- **Choose your timing wisely.** If your rider is across the arena, screaming won't help them, it'll just distract everyone.
- **Stay composed.** Your rider feeds off your energy. If you're panicked and frantic, guess what? They will be too.
- **Lead with professionalism.** Model the kind of sportsmanship you want your riders to emulate.

CALM IS CONTAGIOUS

Your energy on the rail is contagious. If you're cool, collected, and focused, your rider will mirror that even from across a crowded arena. If you're red-faced and waving like you're directing an airstrike, don't be surprised if your rider starts looking around in panic, wondering what disaster they missed.

In moments of pressure, your calmness might be the invisible hand that steadies them enough to shine.

BE A FAN, NOT A DISTRACTION: SPECTATOR ETIQUETTE THAT MATTERS

Let's talk about one of the fastest ways to ruin a ride and a class you're not even in: startling a horse from the rail.

It sounds ridiculous until you've watched a beautiful ride unravel because someone in a chair decided to wave at their cousin across the ring or couldn't figure out how to quietly fold their seat without sounding like they were wrestling an aluminum ladder.

Yes, the outside environment is unpredictable. We all get that. But if you're choosing to sit ringside, front row to the action, you've also taken on a small but mighty role in the performance. And that role is *not* air traffic controller.

Spectators have startled horses by: Clapping at the wrong time, tossing jackets over the rail, standing suddenly during a pass, fidgeting like their chair is trying to escape, waving arms like they're guiding in a 747 and pretty much anything else you can imagine.

What might seem like innocent movement can have major consequences. One startled jump. One break in gait. One blown lead. That horse loses the class, the rider's hours of work go unrewarded, and a moment of potential greatness is gone.

What makes it even worse is that it was completely preventable. Judges want to find a winner. We come into the ring ready to reward the best performance. But when an outside, unnecessary distraction robs a rider of that chance? It's frustrating. And yes, we remember. We remember the moment. We remember the rider's heartbreak. And often, we remember what you looked like when it happened.

So if you're going to watch from the rail, here's the golden rule: **Be a fan. Not a distraction.**

Cheer with purpose. Sit still with awareness. Respect the space like it's part of the show because it is. If you're serious about supporting great horsemanship, act like it.

WHY IT MATTERS

At the end of the day, coaching from the rail isn't just about helping your rider, it's about representing your barn, your professionalism, and the future of the sport.

When we show composure, focus, and pride, we lift the entire class and the entire sport higher.

"The goal isn't to blend into the background. The goal is to elevate the rider so seamlessly that the spotlight never leaves them."

When in doubt, remember: your presence matters. Use it wisely.

Before you head to the rail, ask yourself:

- Would I want my behavior filmed and played back on a Jumbotron?
- Am I coaching or am I narrating every breath my rider takes?
- Am I building confidence or creating drama?

If in doubt, breathe deep, stand tall, and remember, your poise might be the strongest coaching tool you have.

29

YOU'RE NOT SHOWING ALONE AND HOW THE ENTIRE ECOSYSTEM IMPACTS THE RIDE

Riders sometimes believe that once they enter the ring, everything else fades away. That the judge is only looking at the horse, the rider, and the performance at that moment. That's a comforting idea, but it's also incomplete. Judges don't judge in isolation. We judge in context. And while the ride itself always matters most, it is never the only thing happening.

Every class exists within an ecosystem. Trainers, parents, barn mates, the warm-up ring, the rail, the camera phones, and the moments immediately before and after the class all create an atmosphere. Judges are human beings standing in the middle of that environment, tasked with making decisions while processing far more than most exhibitors realize.

This does not mean judges are influenced by drama or theatrics. It does mean that professionalism, composure, and awareness, or the lack of them, are noticed.

Let's break down the ecosystem.

TRAINERS ON THE RAIL

Good trainers add clarity. Excessive rail activity adds noise. Constant motion, visible urgency, or overly animated coaching can unintentionally make a rider look less settled, even when the guidance itself is correct. From the judge's perspective, a rider who appears to rely heavily on real-time instruction often reads as less confident and less independent.

Preparation happens before the class. In the ring, the goal is execution. Support your rider. Coach them. Then trust them to ride.

PARENTS AND "STAGE MOM" ENERGY

Parents want their children to succeed. That's normal. What isn't helpful is turning the rail into a second performance.

Overreactions while filming, visible disappointment, head-shaking, or dramatic responses, positive or negative, pull focus away from the rider and add pressure they don't need.

Judges notice when young riders maintain composure regardless of what's happening on the rail. The calmest adults often raise the most confident riders.

FRIENDS FILMING AND RING-SIDE COMMENTARY

Phones are everywhere now, but they not the issue. Behavior is.

Whispered commentary, audible reactions, or filming with obvious emotional investment can create unnecessary tension. Riders feel it. Horses feel it. Judges see it. If you're filming, do it quietly and respectfully. The ring is not "content time." It's performance time.

BARN ENERGY BEFORE THE CLASS

The tone surrounding a ride matters. When the environment leading up to a class feels steady, organized, and focused, that calm often shows up in the ring. Riders make clearer decisions. Horses stay softer. Nothing feels rushed.

Judges can often tell when a ride is coming from preparation rather than reaction. That difference shows up in the details.

PROTECTING YOUR PEACE AND YOUR ENERGY

The ecosystem doesn't just affect how judges perceive you. It can literally affect how *you ride*.

High-level performance requires focus, emotional regulation, and a certain amount of mental quiet. That doesn't happen by accident. It has to be protected. Riders who consistently perform at their best understand this, even if they've never articulated it that way.

Not everyone around you deserves access to your headspace on show day. Every conversation, comment, facial expression, and last-minute opinion pulls at your attention. Some riders absorb all of it. Others set invisible boundaries and ride as if nothing outside the ring exists. Those riders tend to look calmer, more deliberate, and more confident, even under pressure. From the middle of the ring, that difference is obvious.

Protecting your peace does not mean being cold, rude, or disengaged. It means being selective. It means limiting unnecessary input before you show. It means trusting the preparation you already did instead of reopening decisions ten minutes before you enter the gate. This is where many good riders unravel. They let outside noise override their plan.

Well-meaning barn mates offer opinions. Parents ask questions that don't need answers. Someone mentions how the judge pinned the previous class. Suddenly, the rider is no longer riding the horse they prepared. They're riding the story forming in their head. Elite riders shut that down early.

They keep pre-ride conversations short and purposeful. They do not rehash mistakes from the warm-up. They do not engage in speculation about placings or politics. They do not watch the rail for validation or reassurance. Their energy stays contained, intentional, and forward.

Horses respond to this immediately. A rider who is mentally settled produces a horse that feels easier, quieter, and more rideable. Judges don't know *why* it looks that way. We just see that it does.

Energy management is part of professionalism. If you need hype, get it from your preparation, not the rail. If you need calm, create it by simplifying your surroundings. The ring rewards riders who arrive mentally ready, not emotionally stirred up.

You cannot control the entire ecosystem, but you can control how much of it you let in. The riders who do this well look like they belong. Not because everything went perfectly, but because nothing unnecessary was allowed to interfere. That composure carries weight. And yes, judges notice it.

WARM-UP RING BEHAVIOR

The warm-up ring is one of the most revealing spaces at a horse show. It is also one of my least favorite places on earth. Managing your own horse while navigating other riders, drivers, and support staff camped out in the middle of valuable arena space with grooming supplies spread everywhere is not for the faint of heart. That said, years of surviving warm-up rings, both as an exhibitor and as a coach, have probably made me a better human overall. Or at least a more patient one.

People are almost always nervous in the warm-up ring, and understandably so. You are preparing to enter the show ring while a lot is happening around you. Horses and riders are moving in every direction. There is often a driving class coming up, which adds rolling equipment and tighter traffic patterns to an already crowded space. There is inevitably someone waving their arms at their rider or at a horse in an attempt to get their attention, usually accomplishing the opposite. More often than not, someone has also invited their new, non-horsey significant other into the warm-up ring so they can capture video, which means you are now trying not to run over a person who clearly has no idea they are in danger.

Stress levels rise quickly in this environment, and when they do, people show you exactly who they are. More than once, someone's warm-up ring behavior has shaped my entire opinion of them as a human being.

I understand the pressure. We are all under it. But snapping at your groom, being dismissive to your trainer, or treating other exhibitors like obstacles instead of colleagues is never a good look. It does not make you appear focused or intense. It makes you appear rattled and unmanaged.

Judges do not score the warm-up ring, but we recognize its fingerprints. A thoughtful, efficient, drama-free warm-up often translates to a confident performance in the ring. Preparation should sharpen you, not drain you. If your energy is already spent before you enter the gate, it will show, and not in the way you want.

POST-CLASS REACTIONS

The class is not over when the ride ends.

How riders, trainers, parents, and barn mates respond after the lineup says a great deal. Quiet professionalism after a win. Grace after a loss. Emotional control when expectations aren't met. Big reactions don't help. They don't change the result, and they don't build credibility.

Judges remember exhibitors who understand that reputation is built across many moments, not just winning ones.

WHY THIS MATTERS

None of this replaces performance. A great ride is still a great ride.

But when classes are close, and many are, judges are evaluating polish, preparation, and professionalism alongside execution. The ecosystem around the ride either supports those qualities or undermines them. You are not showing alone.

If you want to stand out for the right reasons, make sure the environment surrounding your ride reflects the standard you want the judge to reward.

When everything else is equal, details matter. And the ecosystem is full of them.

30

BE A GOOD HUMAN. IT PAYS OFF.

We are in a judged sport, but not everything needs your judgment.

Too often, competitive drive spills into how people treat each other once they leave the ring. That is where this sport either strengthens or corrodes. Talent alone does not determine its future. Culture does.

Horse shows are shared spaces. Barn aisles, warm-up rings, in gates, and ringside seats are all classrooms where behavior is learned, modeled, and repeated. The way you speak about others, respond to losses, and acknowledge success contributes to the environment everyone competes in.

Strong programs are built on respect as much as results. Riders who lift others, trainers who protect their culture, and owners who value integrity create ecosystems where people want to stay. Kindness is not softness. It is confidence without insecurity.

When you carry yourself with professionalism and generosity, people notice. Judges notice. Peers notice. Young riders absorb it. Over time, that reputation matters. It influences trust, opportunity, and how you are remembered long after individual results fade.

Choose to compete hard in the ring and act with decency everywhere else. The sport needs both. Being a good human does not take anything away from your performance. It adds to it.

THIS CHAPTER IS MEANT TO BE A MIRROR

This chapter is not here to remind you to be nice. You already know how to do that. It is here to hold up a mirror. To give you a quiet moment to look at how you actually show up when no one is handing you a ribbon. When things go your way. When they don't. When you are tired, frustrated, or feel overlooked.

Mirrors are uncomfortable because they do not argue or reassure. They simply reflect, show patterns, tones, habits and reactions. These are things we often justify in ourselves while judging in others. In a sport where performance is constantly evaluated, it is easy to forget that behavior is being assessed too, just not on a card.

If something in this chapter makes you defensive, pause. That reaction is information. It usually points to an area where growth is still available. This is not about perfection or public virtue. It is about alignment. Making sure the competitor you believe yourself to be matches the professional others experience.

The strongest competitors are not the ones who read this and think:
I already do all of this. They are the ones willing to ask, *Where am I slipping when it would be easier to justify it?*

This level of self-awareness is not soft. It is disciplined and in the long run, it is one of the most competitive advantages you can develop.

WHY THIS MATTERS

Horse shows are not just collections of classes. They are communities where trainers, riders, parents, owners, officials, and volunteers all cross paths every day. Every interaction, whether helpful or harmful, shapes how people experience the sport. If the environment is bitter and ego-driven, riders leave, owners lose interest, and young people drift away. If the environment is supportive, riders stay longer, barns grow, and the sport as a whole flourishes.

You cannot separate competition from culture. The way you treat others becomes part of your reputation and, over time, your legacy.

WHAT IT LOOKS LIKE IN PRACTICE

Support each other. Compliment the rider who nailed their pass. Congratulate a trainer whose horse just looked the best you've ever seen it go.

Help the new kid. Everyone remembers being green. Point them in the right direction, explain the warm-up order, or encourage them when they look overwhelmed.

Fix the small things. If a competitor's number is crooked, straighten it. If a piece of equipment is slipping, point it out. Do not laugh or gossip.

Share strategy when it helps. Sometimes one small piece of insight can give a rider or parent confidence. Hoarding or gatekeeping valuable information helps no one.

These moments are not weakness. They are proof that you understand the sport is bigger than just your own ride.

THE MISCONCEPTION ABOUT KINDNESS

Too many competitors believe that kindness equals softness, that supporting others makes you look less competitive. The opposite is true. The strongest competitors carry themselves with confidence and generosity. They know that lifting the sport does not take anything away from their own chances in the ring.

Being decent does not dilute your edge. It sharpens it. Because when you earn respect for both your results and your character, people notice. And over time, that influence works in your favor.

WHO IS WATCHING

Do not think for one second that it goes unnoticed. Judges see who behaves with integrity in and out of the ring. Owners and parents see how professionals treat each other. Kids in the barn aisle watch how adults act, and they copy it. The next generation is learning the unwritten rules by observing how you carry yourself.

If you gossip, belittle, or undermine, you are giving permission for others to do the same. If you model respect, humility, and generosity, you are building a culture that will last beyond you.

WHAT TO DO ABOUT IT

If we want this sport to thrive with integrity, the work starts now. It starts with you.

- Compliment before you criticize.
- Look for ways to help, even in small gestures.
- Celebrate good riding, no matter the barn colors.
- Set the tone in your own barn by refusing to tolerate disrespect.

Choose generosity over jealousy. Choose respect over ego. Being a good human is not just about doing the right thing, it is also strategic. It makes the sport better for everyone, and it ensures that when people remember you, they remember more than just your ribbons.

This sport does not need more talent without character. It needs competitors who understand that how you win matters. Be ruthless about your preparation. Be disciplined in the ring. And everywhere else, be someone people trust, respect, and want to stand next to. That combination is rare. And it wins more than people realize.

31

WHEN THE HORSE DOESN'T FIT. WHY LETTING GO IS SOMETIMES THE SMARTEST MOVE

"Buying the wrong horse right from the beginning ruins a lot of people. It's not that the horse is bad, it's just a bad fit."
— paraphrased from Clinton Anderson

THE MISMATCH NO ONE WANTS TO ADMIT

There is a moment every good trainer dreads. It is the moment they realize a client's horse is simply the wrong match.

It might be a kind horse, a talented horse, even a winning horse, but it is not the right one for that rider. When the rider, parent, or trainer refuses to acknowledge the mismatch, frustration turns into resentment. What should have been a stepping stone becomes a dead end.

From the middle of the ring, we see this play out all the time. A rider struggling to manage a horse that is too much for them does not just hurt their own confidence. They disrupt the balance of the entire class. It is uncomfortable to watch and nearly impossible to reward. The judging card does not say "wrong horse," but trust me, we are thinking it.

THE DIFFERENT KINDS OF MISMATCHES

Not all mismatches look the same. Some are obvious. Others sneak up on you.

A skill mismatch happens when a green rider is paired with a highly trained, high-octane show horse. A temperament mismatch shows up when a timid rider is paired with a bold, dominant horse, or an aggressive rider is matched with a sensitive one.

A goal mismatch appears when an ambitious rider is mounted on a horse that tops out early, or when a novice rider buys a world-class campaigner that requires finesse they do not yet have. Physical mismatches matter too. Size and strength are not superficial details.

Every version of a mismatch leads to the same outcome: frustration, regression, or someone eventually walking away from the sport altogether.

THE FALSE HOPE TRAP

Clinton Anderson calls this one of the most dangerous mistakes in the horse world. He often uses the example of riders bringing home off-track Thoroughbreds because they are "pretty much free," only to find themselves overwhelmed by a horse trained to run, not listen.

It is like giving a teenager a Ferrari and expecting a smooth Sunday drive.

In the show ring, the version we see is the green rider handed a high-powered five-gaited horse, or the flashy youngster with zero tolerance for amateur mistakes. The sale video looks incredible. The horse has presence, motion, and all the makings of a future champion. But once reality sets in, the rider is overwhelmed, the horse is confused, and both end up worse off. Fear and frustration are the only things showing, and that does not place.

EXCEPTIONS DON'T ERASE THE RULE

Yes, there will always be someone who says, "We made it work." Congratulations. That does not mean the rule does not exist.

Judges do not grade potential. We grade what actually happens in the ring. If a horse is over-faced or underprepared, we see it. No amount of sparkle, bravery, or good intentions can disguise a poor fit.

What often gets missed is that forcing something to "work" usually comes at a cost. The horse loses confidence. The rider starts surviving instead of riding. The picture unravels under pressure. Even if you survive the class, you have taught the horse that the ring is a place where it feels overwhelmed instead of capable.

There is a difference between stretching a horse and exposing one. Progress should look progressive. When the class is right, the horse appears comfortable doing its job. When it is not, the horse looks busy, tense, or reactive and judges will recognize that distinction.

One exceptional outcome does not rewrite the standard. It only proves that someone got lucky once. Sustainable success comes from preparation, timing, and honesty about where the horse truly is. Showing a horse where it can succeed is not playing it safe. It is playing the long game.

CHOOSING THE RIGHT DIVISION AND WHY IT MIGHT NOT BE THE ONE YOU WANT

Sometimes the mismatch is not just the horse and rider. It is the job you are asking the horse to do.

One of the most common mistakes I see from center ring is riders trying to force a horse into a division simply because it is the one they dreamed of showing in. Maybe they grew up watching the Five-Gaited stake class and always pictured themselves making a victory pass to roaring applause. However, if their horse struggles to rack, lacks drive, or does not enjoy the pressure of that division, the gap between dream and reality becomes obvious. From center ring, it is not just disappointing. It is frustrating.

We can tell when a horse is not suited for the job they have been assigned. They may be anxious, flat, or trying their best but still unable to deliver. In those moments, the rider's desire has outweighed the horse's well-being, and it is hard to reward that.

If you cannot be happy showing your horse in the division they truly belong in, it may be time to re-evaluate your plan. It is not failure, it is a fork in the road.

You can adjust your expectations, honor your horse's strengths, and shine in a division that suits them. Or you can place that horse with someone better matched and find a partner who fits your vision. The right division changes everything. The horse lights up. You ride better. The whole picture improves.

When it is not the right fit, it feels like swimming upstream. It is exhausting, disheartening, and usually unrewarded.

THE HIDDEN COSTS OF FORCING IT

The wrong horse does not just waste time. It can leave scars. Confidence erodes when riders constantly feel behind the motion, late to the aid, or physically overmatched. Riders stop trusting themselves. They second-guess every decision. Eventually, they assume the problem is their ability, not the situation.

Good horses suffer too. Horses that are repeatedly corrected, pulled on, overdriven, or misunderstood do not improve. They become defensive. They brace, dull, some shut down completely while others escalate. What started as a mismatch slowly turns into a "problem horse" that did not need to exist.

Financially, forcing it is expensive. Training bills stack up while progress stalls. Vet bills increase. Equipment changes can multiply. Families feel the strain as frustration grows alongside expenses, and the joy that brought everyone into the sport starts to disappear.

These are the hidden costs of refusing to admit what everyone else can already see.

The hardest truth is forcing the wrong fit rarely creates breakthroughs. It creates damage that takes far longer to undo than it would have taken to course-correct early.

Action step: Separate effort from effectiveness. Ask whether the work you are doing is producing consistent improvement or merely consuming time and money. Progress should feel challenging but directional, not chaotic and draining.

SPOTTING THE SIGNS EARLY

A tough ride now and then is normal. Growth is uncomfortable. That is expected. A constant uphill battle is not.

Red flags include anxiety that grows instead of shrinks, resistance that worsens instead of improves, and lessons spent managing behavior issues instead of building skills. When months pass without real breakthroughs despite consistent work, that is not grit. That is information.

Patterns matter more than isolated days. One bad class doesn't necessarily have a larger meaning, however five in a row means something. One rough transition is training. Repeated arguments in the same places point to communication breakdowns, physical limitations, or a fundamental mismatch.

Horses and riders give feedback constantly. Most people ignore it until it becomes impossible to miss.

Action step: Track progress honestly for sixty days. Not feelings. Observable changes. Is the ride becoming calmer, more consistent, and more confident? If not, stop adding pressure and start asking better questions.

THE SUNK COST TRAP

Many riders and owners stay stuck with the wrong horse because admitting a mistake feels worse than continuing to struggle.

"We have already put so much money into this horse."
"If I just try harder, maybe it will click."
"Selling feels like giving up."

None of those statements improve the ride.

The money is already spent. The time is already gone. Continuing does not recover either. It only adds more cost, more frustration, and more emotional wear.

Smart business people cut losses before they compound. Smart horse people do the same. Selling or re-homing the wrong horse is not failure. In fact, it is our responsibility as horse owners to find the best fit or situation for these animals. Often that horse thrives with a different rider, a different program, or different expectations. Meanwhile, the rider regains confidence instead of losing years trying to force alignment.

TRAINERS GET STUCK TOO

Sometimes the rider is not the only one trapped in a bad fit. Trainers get boxed in as well.

A horse may not suit the program, but the trainer keeps pushing to avoid disappointing a client, losing income, or admitting the purchase was wrong. Emotional attachment, financial pressure, or the desire to protect reputation can keep everyone stuck. This is where leadership matters.

When trainers avoid the hard conversation, progress stalls. Lessons turn into damage control. Horses get drilled instead of developed. Riders lose trust. Burnout follows.

The outcome is predictable. Progress stalls and everyone feels the frustration. The horse pays the price mentally or physically or both. It is not fair to the rider. It is not fair to the trainer. And it is certainly not fair to the horse.

Action step: Normalize regular check-ins. Ask directly, "Is this horse still serving the rider's long-term goals?" If the answer becomes unclear, address it early, before it becomes damaged.

THE JUDGE'S TAKE

What most exhibitors do not realize is that mismatches genuinely annoy the judge. Not out of anger, but because they make our job harder.

Judges are there to reward performance, not investment or

potential. When a rider is clearly out-horsed, or a horse is being ridden down to a rider's level, the picture does not add up. It stands out immediately. At the highest levels, these mismatches do not just hurt placings. They damage credibility.

Judges see the full equation: the horse's quality, the rider's skill, and the training behind them. When those pieces do not align, the team stops looking competitive and starts looking mismanaged. That impression lingers far longer than most riders realize.

The right horse makes good riding visible. The wrong horse exposes gaps no amount of effort can hide. The goal is not to make it work at all costs. The goal is to build a partnership where both horse and rider can succeed without damage. Choosing alignment over ego is not quitting. It is leadership.

LETTING GO GRACEFULLY

Letting go of a mismatched horse is not failure. It is wisdom earned through experience.

The hardest part is not the decision itself. It is separating ego from responsibility. Riders often stay stuck because they feel loyal to the investment, the story, or the hope of what the partnership was supposed to become. But hope is not a training plan, and loyalty does not fix misalignment.

The first step is an honest evaluation. Not reassurance. Not encouragement. Truth. Seek out a trainer or professional who has no emotional or financial reason to tell you what you want to hear. Ask direct questions and be willing to act on what you hear. Is this horse suited to my goals? Is this partnership improving, or simply surviving? Are we developing skills, or managing limitations?

Reframe selling or re-homing not as quitting, but as creating opportunity. Many horses that struggle in one program thrive in another. A horse that overwhelms one rider may be perfect for someone else. A horse that resists one style of training may flourish under a different system. Letting go gives the horse a chance to succeed instead of continuing to struggle under pressure it cannot meet.

Grace matters in how you do this. Place the horse thoughtfully. Be honest about strengths and limitations. Match the horse to a rider and program where it can be confident, understood, and successful. That is not giving up. That is good horsemanship.

The right horse brings out your best. It builds confidence instead of draining it. Progress feels challenging but achievable. The partnership moves forward instead of constantly recovering.

The wrong horse keeps you in survival mode. Every ride feels like damage control. Every class feels like a test of endurance instead of expression. No amount of desire can override that reality. Choosing alignment over attachment is one of the most mature decisions a rider can make.

FINAL REFLECTION

Every great rider learns this lesson eventually. The only difference is how long it takes and how much damage happens before they accept it.

Success at the top is not built by forcing bad fits. It is built by assembling the right partnerships at the right time. Riders who reach elite levels understand that progress is not about proving something to others. It is about setting themselves and their horses up to succeed.

Letting go of a horse that does not fit is not a weakness. It is clarity. It is the mark of a rider who understands their goals and respects their limits. It is the mark of a trainer who protects their program and their horses. It is the mark of an owner who values long-term progress over pride and short-term optics.

The wrong horse teaches you clarity. The right horse changes everything. Knowing the difference, and acting on it, is what separates experience from wisdom.

32

THEY'LL NEVER GET IT AND THAT'S OKAY

"You better pick someone that loves what you do. Because horses are a drug. It doesn't wear off, and people that don't have that drug will never understand."
—Clinton Anderson

If you spend enough time in this industry, someone will eventually look at your life and assume you have lost your mind. They will struggle to comprehend why an adult chooses to spend countless hours at a barn instead of doing something more conventional. They will wonder why you sacrifice sleep, comfort, vacations, and disposable income for an activity that demands more than it ever guarantees. They will not understand how you can work a fourteen-hour show day, walk into a restaurant covered in horse hair, and still talk about your ride like it was the highlight of your month. From the outside, none of it looks rational, and that is exactly why most people will never understand it.

The truth is that horse people are wired differently. You do not participate in this world because it makes sense on paper. You participate because something in you comes alive here. You know the pride that comes from earning a ribbon you worked months to achieve. You know the sting of disappointment when a ride goes poorly and you replay it for days. You know the satisfaction of watching a young horse develop strength, confidence, and understanding. You know the specific thrill that comes from partnering with an animal who trusts you enough to carry your goals with you. These experiences are real, powerful, and difficult for outsiders to understand because they have never felt anything close to it.

People who do not live in this world often reduce it to financial cost, inconvenience, and time consumption. They see the scheduling conflicts, the long drives, the early mornings, the missed events, and the money that disappears into training, equipment, entries, and travel. What they do not see is the meaning behind it. They do not see how this lifestyle sharpens your identity. They do not see how it teaches discipline, commitment, resilience, and patience. They do not see how much emotional intelligence is required to communicate with an animal who cannot use words but understands everything. They do not see how much personal integrity is built inside the daily rhythm of training and showing. They do not see any of that because they are not built to recognize it.

When the people closest to you do not understand your commitment, the pressure can feel heavier. A partner may ask why you are leaving again this weekend. A parent may ask whether you will ever slow down. A friend may insist that you make more time for them and treat the barn as something trivial in comparison. It can be frustrating to feel like you must justify something that gives your life direction and meaning. You may feel tempted to defend the costs, the time, and the sacrifices involved. You may want to give a full explanation of what the sport means to you. You do not owe anyone that level of clarification. You are allowed to love something deeply without providing a dissertation every time someone questions it.

You can care about the people in your life while accepting they may never fully understand this part of you. They do not have to understand it in order to respect it. If someone cares about you, they should care about what strengthens you. For many equestrians, horses are not simply an interest. They are the structure around which your goals, work ethic, friendships, and personal growth are built. This is the environment where you feel most capable. It is where you process stress. It is where you push yourself. It is where you find both challenge and relief. Expecting someone outside of this world to feel all of that is unrealistic.

If you are building a life with someone, compatibility matters. A partner does not need to participate in the sport, but they must respect its significance. They must recognize that it is not a passing phase and that it will not "calm down" with age or convenience. They need to understand that this lifestyle affects your schedule, your finances, your priorities, and your emotional investment. A partner who sees the barn as competition will eventually become an obstacle. A partner who treats your passion as a problem will drain your motivation. A partner who tries to restrict your involvement will undermine the foundation of your identity. It is far better to set expectations early and communicate clearly that this life is permanent, intentional, and meaningful.

Most people do not pursue anything that requires the level of responsibility you carry. They do not wake up every day knowing that a thousand-pound athlete depends on them. They do not navigate the challenge of building a physical and mental partnership with an animal whose performance reflects both your strengths and your weaknesses. They do not experience a sport where progress happens slowly, setbacks happen instantly, and both outcomes demand emotional fortitude.

They have never entered a show ring knowing that ninety seconds can summarize months of work. They have never felt the weight of caring deeply about something unpredictable, athletic, sensitive, and completely separate from human logic.

This is why they struggle to understand. They simply do not live in a world that asks this much of them.

Not everyone needs to understand your life, but you must remain committed to it. There is no benefit to pretending horses are a casual interest. There is no value in downplaying your devotion to appear more balanced or agreeable. There is no reason to hide the ambition or joy you feel because someone else finds it excessive. You should continue showing up with the same level of purpose that brought you into this sport. You should accept that your goals require time, effort, and consistency. You should never apologize for loving something that contributes positively to your identity.

Over time, you will naturally build a circle of people who do understand. They may be fellow competitors, longtime barn friends, trainers, or mentors who have lived through the same highs and lows. These are the people who know exactly what you mean when you describe a horse "starting to click." They know how exhausting a setback can be. They know how rewarding a breakthrough feels. You do not need to explain the emotional weight of a show season to them. They understand the pressure, the planning, the disappointment, and the triumph without requiring a translation. This shared understanding creates a community where your intensity is normal, your goals are respected, and your passion is encouraged.

Everyone outside of that circle is allowed to feel confused. Their confusion is not a criticism of your choices. Their lack of understanding does not diminish the value of your commitment. You will come home tired, dirty, sore, and sometimes discouraged, but you will also come home fulfilled. You will return to the barn because it gives you something nothing else can replicate. It gives you purpose, direction, responsibility, athletic challenge, and emotional depth. It gives you a reason to strive for improvement in a world where improvement is never guaranteed but always possible.

This is not simply a sport or a pastime. It is a defining part of who you are. Most people will never understand loving something this deeply, and that is fine. You do not need them to understand it. You only need to continue honoring it. If you are fortunate enough to have something in your life that fuels you this completely, protect it. It is rare to find a passion that shapes your character and strengthens your identity. You have found one. Now hold onto it with conviction and pride.

33

WHAT DOESN'T ANNOY THE JUDGE (AND MIGHT EVEN EARN YOU RESPECT)

It's easy to get wrapped up in what not to do in the show ring. Riders spend hours analyzing every move, worrying they'll do something to rub the judge the wrong way. But here's a truth that might surprise you: many of the things you're overthinking don't bother us at all.

In fact, some of the choices riders make, especially when they're rooted in horsemanship, safety, or strategy, are not only acceptable, they're respected. Judges are horsemen too. We know things don't always go perfectly, and we're not looking for robotic performances. We're looking for smart, prepared riders who show us they understand how to make the best of the moment they're in.

So here are ten things you don't need to stress about. Not only do they not annoy the judge, they might even leave us impressed.

1. One-Horse Classes Aren't Your Fault

We know one-horse classes aren't ideal for anyone, but we also know it's not your fault. Unless you specifically requested the class just to avoid competition (and yes, we do notice when that happens), we respect that you showed up and entered. You deserve our full attention just like everyone else, and we're going to give it. Don't rush or apologize for being the only one.

2. Taking a Moment in a One-Horse Class
If you're the only entry and your horse needs a moment to settle, take it. Judges are horsemen too. We understand that horses have moods, nerves, or off days. If you need an extra minute to settle before lining up or want to wait until you can make a clean transition, do it. As long as you're not holding up the show unnecessarily, we're not annoyed, we're grateful you're doing what it takes to give a fair picture of your horse.

3. Delaying a Transition to Create Separation
Waiting to pick up your canter, trot, or slow gait so you can find your own space? It is, not only okay, it's smart. As long as it's within reason and doesn't disrupt the class, we recognize it as ring strategy. We'd rather you create a clean moment than get caught in a traffic jam.

4. Moving in the Lineup for Safety
When a horse next to you starts acting up and you move away quietly, even if the card isn't in yet, we're not going to penalize you. You're protecting your horse and yourself. That shows maturity, not misconduct.

5. Circling or Cutting Across to Avoid Trouble
Sometimes you need to veer off track to avoid a situation brewing nearby. Whether it's circling or adjusting your path across the ring to steer clear of a horse that's getting worked up, we don't mind. Your awareness and control are appreciated, not penalized.

6. Wearing Older Suits or Equipment

You don't need the newest coat or the latest saddle to be competitive. If your turnout is clean, fits well, and looks intentional, we're good. Quality horsemanship doesn't come with a price tag.

7. Skipping the Bling
We're not judging your lapel pin, bun barrette, or number magnets. Bling is optional. A simple, neat look will never count against you.

8. Carrying (or Not Carrying) a Crop
Your crop is your business. If your horse goes better with one, use it. If they don't need it, leave it behind. That includes equitation. We're not docking points based on what's in your hand, we're watching how you ride.

9. Keeping Your Horse Calm in the Equitation Lineup
When we walk the line in equitation, we're looking at the overall picture, but we're not expecting your horse to stand like a literal statue. If you need to speak softly, lower your hands, or give a quiet pat on the withers to help your horse settle, do it. That's horsemanship. And horsemanship is what we're really judging.

10. Not Smiling the Whole Time
You're not on a pageant stage. We're not expecting a plastered-on smile for the full class. Confidence, connection, and presence matter more than fake cheer. A focused rider with good energy reads much better than someone forcing a grin while they're falling apart inside.

You don't need to be perfect. You just need to be present, aware, and prepared to do what's best for your horse in the moment. Most of the time, judges aren't looking for picture-perfect performances, we're watching for riders who think like horsemen, act like professionals, and handle real-time challenges with poise. So the next time you're in the ring, stop worrying about whether that tiny adjustment annoyed the judge. If it was thoughtful, safe, or strategic, it probably didn't.

Judging isn't glamorous (though we are often in formal attire). It's long hours, tough decisions, and sometimes, angry people. But it's also one of the most educational, humbling, and clarifying experiences I've ever had in this sport.

It sharpened my instincts. It refined my priorities. And it gave me the one thing every competitor wants more of: clarity. I didn't become a judge to hold the power. I became a judge to understand the game. And I'll never look at the show ring the same way again.

34

CENTER RING SECRETS

It is not every day that judges from across our industry sit down to speak openly about their craft. The fact that they agreed to do so here is extraordinary.

Judges are often seen only as the mysterious figures holding a clipboard in center ring, but in this chapter they step out of that role and share the kind of perspective some exhibitors spend a lifetime trying to decode. Their willingness to be candid says something important. The people who guide this sport do not want to simply evaluate it, they want to help it thrive.

At its best, this industry is built on far more than ribbons and trophies. It is built on people who care deeply about the horses, the exhibitors and the future. These interviews are a gift, and if you read with an open mind, they may change the way you enter the ring.

Below are the questions each judge was asked, followed by their responses grouped together so you can easily compare their perspectives. To provide context for the voices you are about to hear, each judge brings a lifetime of experience to this conversation.

Melissa Moore officiating at the World Championship Horse Show. Photo by Julia Shelburne-Hitti.

Melissa Moore is one of the most experienced and respected judges in the American Saddlebred industry, with a depth of judging experience that arguably surpasses anyone currently officiating in the sport. A USEF-licensed judge across multiple divisions, she has officiated at the highest levels for decades. In addition to her judging career, she is a highly accomplished trainer and breeder based in Kentucky, having developed and shown numerous World and National Champions. Quite frankly, Melissa is someone who could have written this book herself. Her willingness to contribute her perspective here is both generous and invaluable.

Jay Wood officiating at the World Championship Horse Show.

JAY WOOD IS a longtime horse trainer, instructor, and a highly experienced USEF-licensed judge in multiple breeds. He has judged the World and National Championships in both Saddlebred and Morgans several times. Based in Minnesota, he owns and operates Westwood Farm. With a career spanning decades, he has trained multiple World Champions. His judging perspective reflects a deep respect for horsemanship, preparation, and consistency in the ring.

Richard Wright, officiating at the Illinois State Fair. Photo by Terry Young.

RICHARD WRIGHT IS a veteran Arabian horse trainer, coach, and licensed judge with more than forty years of experience in the industry. Based in Illinois, he has worked extensively with horses and exhibitors nationwide and has officiated at many premier competitions in Arabians, Morgans and Saddlebreds. His insight is grounded in tradition, breed standards, and practical show-ring judgment. He holds in USEF judges license in a diverse range of show horse breeds.

Jolene Galvin-Yerckie judging Morgan Grand National & World Championship Horse Show. Photo by Howard Schatzberg.

JOLENE GALVIN-YERCKIE IS a USEF-licensed judge and riding instructor with broad experience across Morgan, Saddlebred, Hackney, Roadster, and Equitation divisions. In addition to regularly judging rated, World and National level competitions, she has spent years teaching and developing riders, giving her a well-rounded perspective that bridges education and evaluation.

What is something a rider does in the ring that immediately earns your respect?

Melissa Moore
Confidence. I can tell immediately if a rider came prepared to

win or if they are unsure of themselves. Showing confidence sets the tone for how I evaluate the rider, driver, horse, or pony.

Richard Wright
When a horse and rider enter the ring and there is nothing I would change, meaning they meet or exceed the ideal. That is exciting. This first pass sets the sliding scale in motion for every competitor in the ring.

Jay Wood
When horse and rider come into the ring with extreme power and take command on the first trip. I cannot look away after that.

Jolene Galvin-Yerckie
A well turned out horse and rider/driver combination who enters the arena presenting themselves with confidence will immediately grab my attention. A rider/driver who has horsemanship and is steering their horse will navigate the arena with a purpose.

What is a habit or behavior that quietly drives you crazy?

Melissa Moore
Riding on top of the judge. I hate having to back up to avoid getting run over. I also dislike riders talking loudly to their horses. Quiet communication is fine. Loud commentary makes the team seem less capable.

Richard Wright
A lack of planning that leads to a sloppy or careless turnout. Tack and clothes should be spotless and fitted well ahead of

time. Nothing about a winning performance should look like an unmade bed.

Jay Wood
In a small class with a clear winner, someone who keeps making extra passes instead of lining up and ending the class.

Jolene Galvin-Yerckie
Poor fitting and outdated show clothes. Your appearance is part of your first impression. You do not have to have a custom-riding suit as there are great consignment shops in our industry. Invest in a suit that is made for your body type and find a capable tailor who can alter the suit to give you the perfect tailored look.

Keep your derby and show hats shaped and clean. Make sure they are the correct size and sit correctly on your head.

Are there trends in training, turnout, or show presentation you wish would disappear?

Melissa Moore
Tails lying flat over a horse's back. I remember when very few horses wore a brace and had beautifully set tails. I like a braced tail, but not one flattened over the spine.

Richard Wright
The trend of confusing fast with fancy. If speed destroys balance, cadence, or precision, I am not impressed. Do not write a check with speed your horse cannot cash.

Jay Wood
Tail braces bent so far over the back that the tail is almost flat. I

prefer a straighter tailset with enough feathers to show off the horse's natural flow.

Jolene Galvin-Yerckie
In pleasure classes I like to see a rider's attire complement their horse not be the focus.

Large lapel pins.

Over coaching from outside the arena. This can draw negative attention highlighting the mistakes the combination being judged is making.

How do you approach judging a horse or rider you know personally, whether that connection is positive or complicated?

Melissa Moore
I do not have a problem judging friends or adversaries. I am there to judge the horse, not the person riding or training it. I compare each horse against the others, and the one that fits the specs and does the job best wins.

Richard Wright
My responsibility is to give a clear snapshot of that specific performance. Personal relationships, good or bad, have nothing to do with that job.

Jay Wood
It is difficult because you tend to be tougher on people you know. I remind myself not to beat my friends just to beat them. Tie the correct horse. Give a friend the benefit of the doubt only if they earned it.

Jolene Galvin-Yerckie
Judging our peers comes with the business of judging. As judges we have an ethical responsibility to give everyone an equal and fair evaluation regardless of a personal relationship.

What is one thing you wish every exhibitor understood about the judging process?

Melissa Moore
Judging is really hard. The difference between first and eighth is often extremely small. I have judged Louisville classes where horses that did not get a ribbon were close to winning. You still have to tie the class, even when it is tight.
I wish exhibitors could stand in center ring and try judging a few classes. They would realize how hard it is to tie ten places and how important it is not to ride on top of the judge. A judge cannot see you if you crowd them. Ten feet is good, fifteen is better, and the rail is best if you can find a spot.

Richard Wright
Two things:
First, judges hope every exhibitor has their best performance.

Second, nothing is personal. The placing reflects only what happened in that class and does not speak to anyone's self worth.

Jay Wood
Judges do not see everything. If you timed it, we probably look at any one horse for about forty five seconds total. You must impress quickly and consistently. Judges also truly try hard to do the best job possible, even when mistakes happen.

Jolene Galvin-Yerckie
I wish all exhibitors fully understood the specs of the class they are showing in. I have always thought it would be helpful to have the class specifications on the back of each exhibitor's competition number. The specification being on the back number would be a reminder to the exhibitor of what they are being judged on.

When you enter the show arena remember that you have entered a competition asking to be evaluated on your performance compared to your peers based on the specifications and the judge's opinion on that given day.

There are times that the separation of 2 competitors is so close that it is the smallest detail that separates the two. As judges we are human and put a lot of thought into the choices we make. I carry many of these classes still in my mind today.

Any advice you think equitation riders or their trainers overlook?

Melissa Moore
Many riders hold their hands too high and look perched on the horse. They need to ride as a team.

Richard Wright
In trying so hard to be seen, some riders forget respect for others in the ring. Assertiveness is good, but management of a class that is inconsiderate or even dangerous will drop you dramatically on my card.

Jay Wood
I want to see riders actually ride. Demonstrate real horseman-

ship, not just pose. Trainers who teach the basics produce the riders who excel.

Jolene Galvin-Yerckie
Listen to your horse, they are always communicating to us through their body. Any movement we make is communication. Before correcting your horse ask yourself, are you the one who miscommunicated?

- A good equitation rider can think strategically, make smart decisions in real time, and present their horse to the judge in the best possible way, no matter what's happening in the ring.
- Some riders are more focused on their points in a pattern rather than keeping the horse balanced and relaxed. Know where you are going and how you are getting there before communicating it to the horse. Riders should bridge their communication from one gait to the next. Judges want to see control, manners, or consistency thought out the pattern.
  - Equitation is story telling conveying the impression of effective form and easy control: You get to draw the judge into your story by your rail work. When performing your pattern, you have 100% of the judge's attention on you. This is where your story becomes unmistakably yours. Sell your story to the judge by captivating their attention to your pattern. An even tempo, deliberate accuracy, and transitions placed exactly on point show not just skill, but intention.

Any stories, pet peeves, or memorable judging moments you are willing to share?

Richard Wright

In several instances in my career, I have had the privilege of seeing a rider or driver gather all the energy and enthusiasm that a horse is trying to give to the point where the horse simply levitates. To see all that power contained in a supple hand so that a simple extension of fingers releases that power down the rail never ceases to amaze me.

Jay Wood

2015 Junior Exhibitor Five Gaited Championship at Louisville
He turned around to see The Daily Lottery make one of the most impressive slow gait passes he had ever seen. Even the ringmaster was blown away.

2021 Louisville, Three Year Old Three Gaited
David Cater showed Hallelujah Moment. After pulling and replacing a shoe, the horse delivered an incredible performance.

2021 Stallion Stake
Burt Honaker showed Epoque Kiss for the first time. Jay told Clark Clouse afterward, "I think this is what it must have felt like to judge Skywatch and Imperator." The entire stake was exceptional.

35

WHAT COMES NEXT

By now, you have probably figured out this book was never just about how not to annoy the judge. It was about showing up in the ring with clarity, purpose, and a competitive edge many exhibitors never develop because we don't talk about the subject enough.

You have read the unfiltered version of what it takes to show well. Not the polite version. Not the watered down "sit up straight and smile" version. The real version. You now know what we actually see, what we are thinking, and why results sometimes feel confusing until they suddenly make sense. Once you understand what truly catches a judge's eye, what distracts us, what impresses us, and what separates first from fourth, the entire game changes.

That is the point. This book was not meant to hand you a checklist and pat you on the back. It was meant to wake you up.

I hope you have taken away that winning is not just about having the fanciest horse or the deepest pockets. It is about intention, choices and preparation. The ability to deliver when it matters. The show ring rewards riders who respect the process, respect the sport, and respect the horse.

THIS IS NOT THE END. IT IS THE TURNING POINT.

Maybe this book confirmed things you already sensed. Maybe it confronted you with truths you did not want to admit. Maybe you don't agree with something I have said. Maybe it gave you a few well-earned wins. If so, good. In any case, that means it did its job. It means it started a necessary conversation. Whether you are an amateur chasing your first ribbon, a junior exhibitor with big dreams, or a professional trying to elevate your program, this book was written to help equip you with real tools, strategy and real world insight that has not been compiled into one place before now.

The gap between "good enough" and "undeniable" is rarely talent. It is not always about budget. It is almost never luck. It is about awareness, discipline and repetition. And the ability to make a thousand small choices that eventually add up to the one that matters.

If this book shifted even one part of how you ride, coach, or prepare, then I am glad. If it left you wondering what else you could be doing, then even better. That means you are ready for more.

RAISING THE BAR TOGETHER

The riders I love to watch are not just talented. They are students of the game. They study the ring, the rules, and their own performance. They ask, "Where can I be better?" And they act on the feedback.

They do not rely on hope. They make deliberate choices. They prepare like professionals, even if they are brand new exhibitors showing in the Academy division.

More than anything, they take themselves seriously before expecting anyone else to. These kinds of riders are magnetic.

These riders become dangerous in the best possible way. They are often the ones climbing to the top faster than anyone predicts.

WHY I WROTE THIS BOOK

I did not write this book to vent. I wrote it because I care about this sport enough to tell the truth when it would be easier to stay quiet.

I have been involved in every aspect of this industry, I have worn the exhibitor number more than most people have. I have held the clipboard. I have coached the rider, trained the horse, and stood at the rail with my heart in my throat. I know how much pressure riders feel and how little real guidance people receive from actual judges when it comes to judged competition.

That is why this book exists. It is a handbook for showing smarter. A reality check for riders who want to win without the drama. A roadmap for anyone who wants to level up without losing the fun.

AND IF YOU ARE STILL WITH ME

Maybe I will see you at a clinic. Maybe I will be judging your next show. Maybe you will be the rider who catches my eye for all the right reasons. Maybe you will be the one who nails the class that has always slipped away. Or maybe you will be the rider who finally feels like everything you have been working toward is starting to land.

Whatever comes next, keep riding with purpose. Keep sharpening your edge. Keep studying the game until you can play it better than anyone else in the ring. And above all, keep showing up for your horse, for yourself, and for the competitor you know you are capable of becoming.

You do not need permission to ride like a winner. You only need to decide that you are done riding like anything less.

See you in the lineup.

Allison Deardorff

2024 South African National Championship in Bloemfontein. From left to right: John Warner, Allison Deardorff, Kelly Hulse, Clark Clouse.

ACKNOWLEDGMENTS

This book would not exist without the people who challenged my thinking, sharpened my voice, and pushed me to say what a lot of people only think.

My deepest gratitude goes to **Sandy Backer, Tina Sutter**, and of course, my mother, **Brooke Deardorff**, whose editorial insight, honesty, and patience helped turn years of experience into something readable, direct, and useful.

Johnny Jones, who not only, gave me a job, but showed extraordinary patience with a young horse trainer right out of college. He gave me ample opportunity to mess up, learn from my mistakes. And I have to acknowledge the full-circle moment when we both judged Louisville for the first time together.

And to my late grandparents, **Willard and Betty Deardorff**. Without their love, work ethic, and dedication to their horses and their family, my career nor writing this book would have been possible.

To all **the riders, trainers, and industry professionals** who trusted me with their questions, frustrations, and ambition over the years: you shaped this book more than you realize. Every chapter exists because someone cared enough to ask how to be better.

Allison's grandfather, Willard Deardorff was the proud breeder of the highly successful gray Five Gaited horse, WCC CH Doubletrees Steel The Show as a weanling.

ABOUT THE AUTHOR

Allison judging the 2025 Mercer County Fair Horse Show. Photo by Avis Girdler.

Allison Deardorff is a lifelong member of the show horse community and a third-generation horseman. She is a nationally respected horse trainer, coach, and multi-breed judge whose career spans decades in the center of the Saddlebred industry and beyond.

She is a graduate of William Woods University, where she studied under renowned Saddle Seat instructor Gayle Lampe.

Allison majored in Political Science and Spanish, with a minor in Equestrian Science.

While still in college, she worked at the highly regarded Callaway Hills Stable under Bob Brison and Burt Honaker and also trained with widely respected trainer, Virgil Helm, taking away invaluable knowledge and skills from these opportunities. She later earned her Master's Degree in Business Administration while training horses full time, combining real-world industry experience with formal business education.

Following college, Allison worked for John T. Jones at Rosemont Manor, where she gained extensive hands-on experience with numerous young horses while guided and taught by John T., whose reputation in the Saddlebred industry speaks for itself. This experience further refined her approach to training, preparation, and long-term horse development.

Today, Allison owns and operates two training operations, one in Oregon and one in Kentucky, alongside her father, UPHA Tom Moore Hall of Fame member Don Deardorff. Known for her sharp eye, high standards, and consistent results, she has trained and shown world-class Saddlebreds and coached riders of all levels to the top of the sport.

She holds USEF Large R judge's cards in American Saddlebred, Hackney, Roadster, Saddle Seat Equitation, and Morgan, and has judged some of the most prestigious competitions in the industry, including the World's Championship Horse Show, the Morgan Grand National & World Championship Horse Show, and the South African National Championship Horse Show. While she has held her judge's cards for over fifteen years, her training career began long before that, giving her a rare dual perspective that sets her apart in the industry.

In addition to her work in the training barn and center ring, Allison has played an active leadership role in the sport. She currently serves as Vice President of the American Saddlebred Horse & Breeders Association Board of Directors and has previously served as Chairperson of United Professional Horseman's Association Chapter Two. She also spent thirteen years on the Northwest Saddlebred Association Board of Directors in various roles, including President. These experiences have given her a broad, behind-the-scenes perspective on the industry that few competitors or judges ever see.

Allison is fiercely committed to raising the bar for horsemanship, rider mindset, and professionalism, both inside and outside the ring. This book brings together lessons learned from the judge's card, the training barn, and decades in the spotlight, designed to help exhibitors stop guessing and start winning.

APPENDIX

This section is for riders, trainers, and professionals who want to go deeper, grow further, or step into leadership roles within our sport. Whether you're looking for practical tools, inspiration, or your next calling, these resources are here for you.

APPENDIX A: HOW TO GET YOUR JUDGE'S CARD

In Chapter Twenty, I suggested those who wanted to learn about what they are being on should attend Judge's School. Here is the information.

Not long ago, I was asked to recommend licensed judges for an upcoming show. I pulled up the list and started scanning through names, only to realize just how short that list really is. While there are some truly excellent judges currently licensed, people who are fair, sharp, and knowledgeable, the pool of active officials is not nearly as large as most people think. In fact, I can easily name at least ten respected professionals in our industry who should be judging but do not hold a card. If you feel called out while reading this, good! For some, it is a matter of time. For others, it is simply something they have never pursued. For our sport to continue evolving in a healthy and credible direction, we need more qualified people stepping into center ring.

If you are a professional trainer, a knowledgeable amateur, a young up-and-comer, or someone who understands the nuances of this sport and cares deeply about it, you should at least consider getting your judge's card. Even if the idea has only crossed your mind once or twice, I want you to take this as your official sign to look into it. I realize judging is not for everyone, but if there is even a flicker of interest, it is worth exploring. The future of the sport depends on honest, experienced horse people being willing to serve in this role.

The process of becoming a licensed official can seem daunting at first, and I have heard plenty of the common concerns. "What if I go through all that work and never get hired?" "What if people think I am not qualified?" These are valid thoughts, but I want you to know that you will not be doing it alone. There are plenty of us, myself included, who are happy to help guide you, answer your questions, and support you through the licensing process. And yes, there are opportunities out there. Good show managers are always looking for new faces who bring fairness, integrity, and a sharp eye to the ring. The industry is stronger when more high-caliber horsemen and horsewomen step up to judge.

Getting your judge's card is not just about giving back to the sport. It will also make you better. Judging changes your perspective in ways that are hard to describe until you have sat in that chair. It gives you a deeper understanding of what actually matters in a class. You begin to see patterns in riding, presentation, and ring strategy. You watch classes unfold from a new angle, both literally and mentally. That perspective will help you grow not only as a professional but also as an exhibitor, trainer, and coach. You will start to understand why certain placings fall the way they do, and you will learn to view classes through the lens of logic and structure rather than just emotion.

Licensed official Emma Caruso, a young professional who is already making an impact as a judge, said it best:

"Judging has helped me grow as a trainer, exhibitor, and promoter of our show horse breeds. Standing in center ring gives you a completely different perspective, and you learn so much. I feel that encouraging more people to judge, especially those of a younger generation, is vital to keeping the industry alive and thriving. I have made great connections, traveled to places I never would have gone, and I am so grateful for the opportunity to be a licensed official."

Emma's experience is proof of what is possible when someone takes the leap. Not only in terms of growth, but in how judging expands your network and helps you connect with others across the country. Whether your goal is to judge a few local shows or eventually be center ring at a national event, your voice and perspective are needed.

And if you are reading this thinking I am talking about you, I probably am. I will not name names, but you know who you are. I have already harassed a few of you lately, and I am not afraid to reach out and do it again. The bottom line is simple. If you care about this industry, if you want to improve it, and if you feel even slightly called to judge, go for it.

Get your judge's card. We need you.

- Become a USEF Licensed Judge: https://www.usef.org/compete/resources-forms/licensed-officials/become-licensed
- Become an Equine Sports Council Certified Judge: https://equinesportscouncil.org/certifiedofficials/

- Information on Saddlebred/Hackney/Roadster and Saddle Seat Equitation Licenses: https://www.saddlebred.com/membership/initiatives/judges-education
- Information on Morgan License: https://www.morganhorse.com/media-events/competitions/judging/
- Information on Arabian License: https://www.arabianhorses.org/judges-stewards/judge/

APPENDIX B: NATIONAL HORSEMAN'S GOPRO VIDEO WITH BEAUTY MARC

Title: *WC Beauty Marc & Allison Deardorff*
Creator / Channel: National Horseman
Platform: YouTube
Published: August 23, 2021
URL: https://youtu.be/Yovx8UD5R8o
Description:
As referred to in Chapter Seventeen, this is the GoPro footage capturing the ride of Beauty Marc and Allison Deardorff during the Kentucky County Fair Three-Gaited Championship, placing Top 3 on the first Saturday night of the 2021 World's Championship Horse Show. The video documents both the performance and the result, offering an unfiltered look at a high-pressure championship moment that continues to resonate within the sport.

Beauty Marc was owned by SG Equine Ventures (Sandy Gallagher) at the time of filming.
Filmed by National Horseman with special thanks to Deardorff Stable, Allison Deardorff, and Sandy Gallagher.

APPENDIX C: HOW TO STUDY THE GAME

A. Video Review and Ring Strategy

The following links are to the websites of the most commonly used horse show videographers. These platforms allow exhibitors to watch full horse show replays or specific classes as a strategic learning tool. Reviewing class videos helps riders and trainers study ring strategy, technical execution, class flow, and judge preferences and behaviors.

In addition, most videographers offer the option to pre-order personalized class videos prior to a show. These recordings can be invaluable for post-show review, skill development, and long-term improvement when used intentionally.

Referenced Videographers:

- **Richfield Video:** https://www.richfieldvideo.com/
- **See Horse Video:** https://seehorsevideo.com/

B. Know the Rules You Are Being Judged By

Understanding the official rulebooks is a critical but often overlooked part of competitive preparation. Judges are required to place classes according to these standards, and riders who understand the rules gain a measurable strategic advantage.

The following resources provide the current rules governing judged competition and class specifications:

- United States Equestrian Federation (USEF) Rulebook: https://www.usef.org/compete/regulation/rulebook
- Equine Sports Council (ESC) Rulebook: https://equinesportscouncil.org/rules/

These rulebooks define class requirements, judging criteria, penalties, and procedural expectations. Studying them alongside video review allows riders and trainers to align preparation, presentation, and strategy with how classes are actually evaluated.

APPENDIX D: RECOMMENDED READING

This book was never intended to teach the fundamentals of riding or how to train a horse. That work has already been done and done exceptionally well. For riders who want to deepen their technical foundation, the following books remain the gold standard within the Saddle Seat industry. These resources pair perfectly with the mindset, strategy, and judge's-eye perspective you've learned here.

Saddle Seat Horsemanship

by Smith Lilly

If you want a comprehensive breakdown of correct Saddle Seat riding and horsemanship, this is the book. Smith Lilly lays out the fundamentals clearly and methodically. This text has become a cornerstone of the industry for good reason.

- Available through the American Saddlebred Museum: https://shop.asbmuseum.org/products/saddle-seat-horsemanship
- Available through Saddle & Bridle: https://saddleandbridle.com/e/all-products/saddle-seat-horsemanship-by-smith-lilly-hardcover
- Available through Fennell's: https://fennells.com/shop/saddle-seat-horsemanship-by-smith-lilly/

Saddle Seat Equitation

by Helen Crabtree

As referenced in Chapter Twenty-Seven, this is the definitive guide to equitation. Helen Crabtree is widely regarded as the authority on correct position, effectiveness, and refinement. If equitation is your focus, start here.

- Available through Saddle & Bridle: https://saddleandbridle.com/e/all-products/saddle-seat-equitation-the-definitive-guide-by-helen-crabtree

Riding for Success: Both In and Out of the Show Ring

by Gayle Lampe

Written by my college professor at William Woods University, this book truly covers the journey from your first ride through the show ring. It bridges horsemanship, rider development, and competition in a way few books manage to do.

- Available through Saddle & Bridle: https://saddleandbridle.com/e/all-products/riding-for-success-both-in-and-out-of-the-show-ring-revised-by-gayle-lampe-paperback
- Available through the American Saddlebred Museum: https://shop.asbmuseum.org/products/riding-for-success-both-in-and-out-of-the-show-ring?srsltid=AfmBOoqm7vLCBsfSLIaNYs4tdtZoDf-khZzW4oXKNDbLqxnadoabErow

APPENDIX E: RING RESETS

10 Things That Require Zero Talent

A downloadable version of this page is available for digital readers: https://drive.google.com/file/d/1hORMiatnexXviAKCIjFqkB3BLJEaPTCH/view?usp=sharing

One Minute Show Ring Affirmations

A downloadable version of this page is available for digital readers: https://drive.google.com/file/d/1yFcxbrfqXOOM2NjYPg4It7DZHm9GSRro/view?usp=drive_link